Homosexuality, Marriage and Society

Shimon Cowen

Published in 2016 by Connor Court Publishing Pty Ltd

Copyright © S. D. Cowen, 2016

All rights reserved. No part of this book may be reproduced or transmitted in any form or by any means, electronic or mechanical, including photocopying, recording or by any information storage and retrieval system, without prior permission in writing from the publisher.

Connor Court Publishing Pty Ltd
PO Box 7257
Redland Bay QLD 4165
sales@connorcourt.com
www.connorcourt.com
Phone 0497-900-685

ISBN: 978-1-925501-11-7

Cover design: Manfred Cohen, manfred@bluesquarecreative.com.au

Printed in Australia

Contents

	Preface	5
1	Same-sex marriage: a struggle of world-views	7
2	Homosexuality and the human being	23
3	Homosexuality and the family	41
4	The same-sex marriage movement and the homosexual	57
5	The same-sex marriage movement and the education of children	75
	Further Reading	93

Preface

The debate over same-sex marriage is really about the human being. It is not about a specific group of persons, but about each and every one of us: what we are, can be, and should be. It does not fit within the right-left divide of politics, but within the conflict of two views of the human being, both of which presently have support on the right and the left. The question is rather, which of these two views should be the moral perimeter or moral constitution of right-left politics in general.

This book had to be assembled quickly in response to the initiative of Connor Court Publishing that it contribute to a full Australian discussion of same-sex marriage within the short interval of time available before major political decisions are made. Accordingly, I have drawn largely on pieces which I have previously written, cutting and pasting (often verbatim), connecting, editing and supplementing them into a whole. The following are the pieces, from which parts have been stitched to form this work: "Submission to the Australian Human Rights Commission on 'Protection from discrimination on the basis of sexual orientation and sex and/or gender identity'" (2010); 'The homosexual anti-bullying program for schools', *Interface*, Vols 4-5 (2010-2014) (first published in the AFA [Australian Family Association] Journal, Vol. 32, No.2, 2011); "'Homosexuality, marriage and society' *Interface*, Vols 4-5 (2010-2014); 'Submission to Review of the National Curriculum', Interface, Vols 4-5 (2010-2014); 'There is more than this...', *Journal of Judaism and Civilization,* Vol. 10, 2014; 'Psychology and the concept of the human being. Rabbi Shimon Cowen in discussion with Professor Stanton Jones', *Journal of Judaism and Civilization,* Vol. 10, 2014; "Politics and reparative therapy", *Journal of Judaism and Civilization,* Vol. 10, 2014; 'Why should a kid pay for a ride on a train? An argument for a religious edcuation', Yeshivah Shul Magazine (Shavuot 2014); and 'Risks to Democracy, Rights in Health Complaints Bill', *News Weekly,* March 26,

2016.

I wish to express my gratitude to Dr Anthony Cappello of Connor Court Publishing for upholding the old-fashioned idea that publishing is primarily about putting out ideas, and doing so with courage and integrity. This is the second time that I have benefitted from his support.

My wife, Miriam, has made many valuable corrections to this book. The haste of getting it ready for publication kept me from incorporating more.

In the spirit of the opening words of this Preface, this book is dedicated to what used to be called "everyman" – to all human beings, in their essential humanity.

1

Same-sex marriage: a struggle of world-views

Overview

The debate over same-sex marriage is in reality a struggle between two world-views. One, the Abrahamic faith tradition (known in our society as the Judeo-Christian ethic), understands the human being as having foremost a spiritual dimension, with an objective and eternal moral compass, that defines stable boundaries for human conduct. The other is the world-view of hedonistic materialism, which grasps the human being primarily as a physical being, entitled to cross traditional boundaries in the quest for gratification. The boundary-crossing in question is same-sex marriage.

The principal issues in the debate follow from the different starting points. First, if sexual relationships are solely a matter of contract between physical persons, then consent justifies variations, as it does altering their property relationships. If, on the other hand, sexual relationships have to do also with a spiritual and ethical mission to propagate generations with full biological identity and ties, traditional marriage cannot be varied by consent. Second, if the physical dimension is primary, homosexuality might be something which defines a person. But if the primary person is spirit or conscience, then homosexuality is something external, encountering and conflicting with that essence from other – physical, psychological and cultural – sources. Third, if the physical is primary, then a variety of sexual impulses might deserve equal satisfaction. But if the spiritual is primary, then the norms of conscience will decide between impulses as to which may be satisfied.

"Compassion" fuels the same-sex marriage debate, but the question is whether compassion can be derailed and tip over into policies which actually harm the family, the homosexual him- or herself, and the education of children.

A conflict of world-views

Two views of the world and the human being

The conflict over same-sex marriage is one – and a key – battle in the struggle for our society and culture between two world-views: the Abrahamic faith tradition, often called in the Australian context the Judeo-Christian ethic, and what has been termed hedonistic materialism.[1] This book takes up the standpoint of the Abrahamic faith tradition, which is the background and moral underpinning of our society and most of world society. Particularly Judaism, Christianity and Islam acknowledge and accept the Abrahamic moral code, known also as the Noahide laws[2], after his predecessor Noah. These laws were reiterated at Mt Sinai. By another route the Abrahamic tradition is also connected with the great religions of the East, Hinduism and Buddhism.[3] The Abrahamic teaching understands every human being to be made in the image of G-d. What this means is that the human being has a soul, which (however unconscious or repressed) is alive to the Divine and mirrors the Divine. It possesses in microcosm and on a human scale, the Divine attributes – G-d's kindness, judgment and so forth – and resonates with the basic values and norms which translate those attributes into ethical conduct, the core code of the Noahide laws at the root of the great world religions.

The Abrahamic faith tradition knows that the human soul is encased in a body, which is driven by many and diverse impulses and instincts. The soul – called by some the conscience of the human being – is the highest and the rightfully sovereign power within the person. Unlike the body, it is not driven. Its task is rather to inform body (the "heart") and mind how to discern amongst the many physical and emotional impulses in the human being: to check those which are unacceptable; to determine which are acceptable, and to empower the person to the modification and

---

1 In my book *Politics and Universal Ethics*, Ballan: Connor Court Publishing, 2011 (elaborated in Chapter 1).
2 See the discussion of these laws in S. D. Cowen, *The Theory and Practice of Universal Ethics*, NY: Institute for Judaism and Civilization, 2014.
3 *Ibid.*, pp. 4-5.

transformation of impulses in accordance with moral norms. This essential, spiritual faculty of the person must muster and marshal body and mind to its directives. In the terms of the great psychologist Viktor Frankl, it "has" them as its vehicles and they need to harmonize with its purposes.

A fundamental department of human ethical conduct is that of sexual behaviour. In the tradition which links Noah, Abraham and the revelation at Sinai (which took place over 3000 years ago) down to the present, four categories of sexual behaviour are prohibited: adultery, homosexuality, bestiality and incest. The Creator, who fashioned the human being, excluded each of these practices as contrary to the Divine image or moral compass within the human being. The biblical verse enjoins a man "to leave his father and mother and cleave to his wife and they shall become one flesh".[4] That "one flesh" is the child which expresses the union of husband and wife and only the unions which can (theoretically at least) produce their own biological offspring in a committed relationship are the Divinely sanctioned ones: not the union of two men or two women, not the union of a human and an animal. Some heterosexual unions are also prohibited because they are incestuous or adulterous.

Our society and societies around the world are faced by the offensive of another world-view, hedonistic materialism. It replaces the shared core beliefs (the Noahide Laws) of the major religions making up Australian society with what traditional religion could easily classify as an "idolatry". Idolatry takes something which G-d has created – be it the sun or something else – and seeks to replace G-d by making this "thing" the ultimate principle of reality. Not only primitive peoples but also secular doctrines of the Enlightenment have produced their versions of idolatry. Such is a purely "naturalistic" view of the world: taking something which G-d had created – "matter" – and making this an Absolute. Physical nature thus becomes "all there is" and "all that ever was and will be". "Pure" secular Marxism is an instance of such an idolatry. Its materialism, which captured Russia, Eastern Europe and China, repressed the old religions and replaced them with its materialistic world-view and the attendant morality of the idol of "historical nature". Atheism of this kind is an idolatry of matter, of the

---
4 Genesis 2:24.

material and the physical alone.

The materialism of many proponents of the modern movement which drives to validate homosexual behaviour is a hedonistic materialism. Not the dialectical materialism (DiaMat) of Communism, but the hedonistic materialism (which I have called "HedonoMat"), which melds the instinct-based psychologism of Freud with materialism. This is a view of the human being as a higher animal in the sentient commonwealth of nature with its program of instinctual gratification for all. It has driven out the great G-d from nature and the small G-d, the soul, from the human being. Without the soul, fixed on G-d to monitor human conduct according to an objective and universal morality, hedonistic materialism provides for the gratification of polymorphous and polymorphing instinct. The gratification of homosexual impulse and now its ultimate legitimation and enshrinement in marriage is part of its ethic.

A basic concept of the world-view of hedonistic materialism is that of humans as supremely entitled to physical pleasure and enjoyment. The secular ideal of human autonomy is now grasped not merely, as the European Enlightenment understood it, as the autonomy of the mind (as the philosopher Kant said, "Have courage to use your own understanding"), but the autonomy of the body. This belief holds that the material flesh of humans should not be constrained in its gratification except where it stops another person's equally free enjoyment of pleasures (or where there is a power asymmetry in the pursuit of pleasure, such as in a sexual relationship of adults and children, or a non-consensual adult sexual relationship). According to this teaching, sexual morality is polymorphous. No one should dictate boundaries on personal and private conduct. To the contrary, it is the duty of the State to facilitate polymorphous self-gratification where the parties are equal and consenting.

Law as society's statement of its values

The question of whether sexual morality is something which government and legislation should back up, or which it should legislatively deregulate, leaving it as a personal and private matter, was at issue fifty years ago in a debate over the Wolfenden Report on "Homosexual offences and Prostitution" in England. Then it had to do with legalization of both. Two sides were formed over the issue. One held that sexual morality was not the State's business and it should allow consenting adults to do what they wanted in their private lives. That position was taken up a prominent Oxford jurist H. L. A. Hart. The English Judge, Lord Patrick Devlin, espoused the other position, which I think most people of traditional faith uphold.

Devlin argued that when Governments and legislatures deregulate matters of sexual morality, they do *not* leave this as a merely personal and discretionary matter, which should not worry people who continue to adhere to traditional morality. Rather, when government legislates to legitimate, condone or support a variant aspect of sexual morality, *society* is in fact making a statement about its values as a whole. Legislation, which endorses certain sexual behaviours, *effectively* teaches them and installs them as social norms. Society and law may not always be able to police morality. Devlin argued that adultery is an example: it is not feasible in our society to prosecute this. But by the same token, society does not have to facilitate, protect and reward adultery. The same applied to homosexual practice. It can either prosecute or tolerate or support a behaviour, and there are great differences between these, as we see in the case of homosexuality. Even those who, as our faith traditions teach us, believe homosexual conduct to be wrong, might agree that, under present circumstances — especially where spiritual literacy and awareness of universal values are weak — it should not be prosecuted. But there is a vast step from not prosecuting to supporting its practice. And that is where legislation and governmental practice have gone: the support of homosexual behaviour in education, legislation and IVF and adoption services, and now the attempt to provide homosexual marriage, effectively *promote it as a* social norm and a cultural value.

The struggle of hedonistic materialism with the Abrahamic faith tradition over same sex-marriage is thus not only a struggle of ideas and values. It is an attempt to accomplish the practical legitimation of homosexual behaviour by legislation, judicial precedent, institutional regulation and childhood education. In fact hedonistic materialism goes beyond the promotion of homosexuality. It is part of a broader deregulation of sexuality, which makes all identities fluid. Its "transgenderist" arm requires that biological men should be allowed to use womens' toilets if they identify as women and biological women should be able to use mens' toilets if they identify as men and that all, including children, should be fully facilitated in sexual reassignment surgery if they want it. The struggle over same-sex marriage is part of a broader argument about what a human being and what society *are and whether and how they can or should be remade.*

The principal issues

Sexuality and human identity

Traditionally, morality has been understood to operate in two dimensions: between person and person and between the individual person and G-d[5]. The interpersonal realm is ethically concerned with prohibitions on harm to another human being. In the realm between the individual person and G-d, or the personal realm, obviously issues such as the belief in, and reverence for, G-d are present. But there is also another aspect of this dimension: human sexuality. Starkly put, sexual morality, with its imperatives and prohibitions, has to do with one's relationship with G-d .

This is a topic which we shall discuss at greater length in Chapter 3, but needs briefly to be explained here. The Abrahamic faith tradition understands the human being as being charged to live ethically according to the universal ethics, through which the soul imitates its Creator. This is a continuing human intergenerational mission. I must be a good person and "make" another good person, my child. That happens when I marry and have children and try to raise them well. Important conditions are

---

5 Adultery additionally affects *another person* in his or her marriage.

involved here: these children need in the first instance be the biological children of my spouse and myself, and to be raised by both of us. There are several reasons for this. One is that the biological nexus of parents and children is vital for human identity. Parents extend their own spiritual identity to their children and children know themselves – acquire identity, with the admixture of their own individuality – as children of their parents. Secondly, the distinct and complementary roles of father and mother are crucial to the education and nurture of that spiritual-ethical identity in their children.

Homosexual marriage cannot fully supply either of these conditions of the human identity: the continuous biological-spiritual identity of generations and the unique roles of the mother and father in its cultivation in the next generation. It calls necessarily for donor gametes and/or surrogacy, so that the offspring are never raised by, and may not even know, both their biological parents. It also takes away from the so-engendered offspring the important combination of fathering and mothering. The result is the creation of a disadvantaged human identity, both in terms of its needs and cultivation as a human potentiality.

It follows that the arguments of "consent" and "victimlessness" in homosexual marriage are irrelevant. Between persons, and in relation to their material property, one can speak of contract or "consent" – to waive entitlements to one's property or allow it to be harmed. If I do not give that consent, then I am the "victim" of the other who harmed my property. With regard, however, to personal identity, who I am and what my purpose is – including the physical and spiritual propagation of a new generation with complete and properly cultivated identity – this is not something from which I can remove myself by contract or "consent". It has to do with my relationship with, and moral charge from, G-d. There is no human being – not I, nor anyone else, nor the unborn child – who may consent to its abrogation.

Human autonomy and responsibility

One of the arguments used to legitimate homosexual conduct all the way through to its enshrinement in marriage is that homosexuality is an inborn characteristic and so needs and deserves expression. There are two issues here. One is whether and to what extent homosexuality is indeed an inborn characteristic. But even deeper than this is the question that even were homosexuality in some individuals to be an inborn disposition, whether that would ethically mandate its expression and gratification. In the words of the head of the Human Genome Project, Francis Collins, viewing homosexuality as "a genetic predisposition, [does] not [make it] a predetermination.[6]"

One form of behaviour that receives universal moral condemnation is that of a paedophile acting on his or her predisposition. Yet the American *Diagnostic Statistical Manual* ("DSM"), the so called "bible" of American Psychiatry describes paedophilia as a *sexual orientation* (even though, realizing its consequences, there was a recent scramble to say that this word was a "typographical error"). The DSM describes paedophilia as an intense and recurrent sexual interest in prepubescent children, which becomes a disorder if it causes a person "marked distress or interpersonal difficulty" or if the person acts on his or her disposition.

There is a website for individuals who possess, but seek to control, this predisposition or orientation, entitled "Virtuous Pedophiles" (www.virped.org). On the website, a Professor of Psychiatry at the University of Toronto, Dr Ray Blanchard is quoted as saying:

> People do not choose to be attracted to children or adults any more than they choose to be attracted to males or females. Not all pedophiles are child molesters (or vice versa). Child molesters are defined by their acts; pedophiles are defined by their desires. There are pedophiles and hebephiles who never act on their sexual attraction towards children. They cannot be blamed for what they feel, and they should be supported for the constant self-restraint they must exercise in order to behave ethically.

---

6 Collins F., *The Language of G-d: A Scientist Presents Evidence for Belief*, New York: Free Press, 2007, p.260 and p.263.

In short, paedophiles are expected to do battle with a deep-seated predisposition towards sexual activity with children. Most people would not exonerate paedophiles were they to indulge that deep-seated – call it even "hard-wired" – drive. Indeed, our society seeks to punish them severely.

If possessing a deep-seated sexual orientation, paedophilia, does not justify the expression of that orientation in practice, why is the argument of "born that way" *per se* used to validate homosexual practice? One explanation is that the proponents of this argument have simply not thought of this contradiction. Another way of explaining the difference is that to follow a paedophiliac disposition involves a victim: the child; to follow a homosexual disposition in a consensual relationship between equals does not. That, however, is an *ethical argument* – not a psychophysical one of "orientation". It however, makes the ethical assumption that consent validates variant sexual relationships. We have already explained why this is false, and most people would agree in the case of an incestuous sexual relationship between consenting adult siblings.

A human being is capable of impulses which run contrary to moral imperatives. Education and personal development include a training in checking, arbitrating and transforming impulse. But it is a profoundly materialistic philosophy – such as that of hedonistic materialism – which says that the impulse *is* the person. Rather, the Abrahamic faith tradition takes up the position, in the words of Viktor Frankl, that the human being exists primarily in the "heights" of the human being – in the human spirit. That spirit is not ruled by impulse and it is the essential and authoritative "I" of the human being. A person can have homosexual impulses, adulterous impulses, incestuous impulses and bestial impulses. None of these make him or her a homosexual, adulterer, incestuous or bestial, unless he or she chooses to act on that impulse. A thief is a person who steals, not who is tempted or has a "drive", however deep-seated, to steal. The human soul is not homosexual, adulterous, incestuous or bestial. It is free of all of these and knows all of these to be inconsistent with its own Divine template. The commonness or the intensity of drives contrary to a Divinely mandated morality do not sanitize or "sanctify" them. However common the "Oedipus complex" Freud found to be in childhood development, that cannot warrant a moral permission for incest. However common the phenomenon of adultery – touted especially by the "celebrity" magazines – might be, that will not produce grounds for legitimating adultery. And however common or strong homosexual impulses may be, that will not of itself make homosexual practice permissible.[7]

This should not come as a surprise. We all know that a child (and an adult too) may be tempted to steal something from a shop. But then something called conscience – if developed in the individual – enters to reject that impulse in the refined human being, based more on principle than fear of being caught. This is exactly the case of the religious person who seeks out therapy for homosexual inclinations. That person's soul or conscience knows that homosexual practice is wrong, and consequently seeks help to restrain or alter that physical impulse. As we shall discuss at length in Chapter 4, contemporary psychiatry and psychology, which for the most part are materialistic and physicalist in their assumptions, do not know what the soul is or seek to iron it out of human personality. That is why they oppose reparative therapy: because they understand homosexuality only as a physical "emergent characteristic" and do not know that the human being also has a soul, the highest and the *essential* faculty of a person. So it is possible that the body might have homosexual predispositions; but the soul, imitating the Divine and the Divine prohibition on homosexual acts, does not. In Chapter 2 we shall see that there is a broad spectrum in the sources and intensity of homosexual inclination – but all are extrinsic to the essential human being: the human soul or conscience. Together with this spectrum and variety of sources of homosexuality go a variety of means available to dealing with it, in accordance with moral autonomy of, and responsibility incumbent upon, the human being.

---

[7] I heard that a young homosexual man, with a sensitivity to the spiritual, put it quite poignantly: "It's wrong to be gay, but it's alright if you are gay". By this he meant that one may – and others should – acknowledge a deep seated homosexual inclination, i.e. "if you *are* gay". At the same time to actualize this in acts which the spiritual tradition has prohibited is not acceptable: "It's wrong to *be* gay". This person also acknowledged a spectrum between the "hard-wired" homosexually inclined person and those with weaker homosexual impulses or experiences for whom a reorientation to heterosexuality in practice is a more easily achievable objective.

"Rights" and "equality"

One of the favourite arguments for the legitimation of homosexual activity all the way through its ultimate enshrinement in marriage is the argument of "rights", with its concomitant slogan of "equality". Opposition to homosexual practice is made out as something akin to racism. This is a deep fallacy. A person can do nothing about the colour of his or her skin and it is something absolutely irrelevant to his or her essential personhood as a spiritual being made in the image of G-d. Recently, under the legislative regime of same-sex marriage in the United Kingdom, a book has been produced for school children, which compares disdain for homosexuality to contempt for the poor. Prince Henry who falls in love with his servant Thomas encounters opposition by his father the King to their "marriage". Prince Henry explains to his father that just as one should not shun a person because he or she is poor, so too Thomas should not be shunned because he is homosexually inclined. This is also a false analogy. Being poor is not a behaviour. Liberal, humanistic strands within religion, which oppose religious orthodoxy, with its concept of objective standards, dress up the same argument in ostensibly religious terms. All human beings, including homosexuals, are made in the image of G-d, they argue, whence homosexuality must also be in the image of G-d. But that is also false. The "image of G-d" refers to the pristine human soul and its ability to resonate with Divine values. It does not refer to the body and its behaviours.

Each human being is judged on the moral merit of his or her conduct and is endowed with the Divine potential to choose and do good. Whilst no one is to be judged for having homosexual or other impulses, carrying homosexual impulse into conscious *practice* is a behaviour, an act, which can be chosen or controlled with or without help sought from others. No person is exempted from moral responsibility merely due to an inclination, no matter how deep-seated (and all the more so when it is less deep-seated). That point was previously made with regard to paedophiliac orientation.

Whilst all human beings factually possess freedom of choice, our freedom is ethically entitled only choose to do good deeds. We are ethically free to perform acts of charity, not to rob banks. Similarly, we have equal entitlements to a choice of *ethical* ends. "Equality" in love may entitle a man to chose from a number of women to marry (and vice versa). It does not entitle him to marry his sister or to have an affair with another man's wife. "Marriage equality" applies only to the range of persons whom it is ethical marry, and according to the Abrahamic faith tradition, that does not apply to a person of the same sex. The naive, *blanket* formula of "marriage equality", being free marry equally whomever one "loves", openly reveals its falsity in Sweden, where incestuous "marriage" exists.

The wrongs of the same-sex marriage movement

False compassion and coercion

Much of the appeal of the same-sex marriage movement is an appeal to "compassion". But what is compassion? Truly compassionate parents know very well that they have to apply "tough love" to children at times. Even though the day of the "rod" is over, the adage "spare the rod and spoil the child" still has a valid application. We have to know how to mix a sense of limits with love, whether in regard to our children or ourselves or others in general. The right mixture of the two is the essence of compassion. Compassion means "I feel for you and even though you have crossed a boundary you shouldn't have, I value and want to help you". True compassion extends love and care, without abandoning boundaries.

The response of the same-sex marriage movement to the suffering of homosexuals presents as universal compassion. Because, there are homosexuals, it argues, who are depressed and even committing suicide, therefore one must embrace homosexuality throughout the institutions and culture of society. This, however, is "love", which demolishes boundaries and in fact harms society. It does not ask, what the sources of dissonance experienced by the homosexual are and whether homosexual relationships in fact are internally dissonant. In fact, the response that social and personal disapprobation of homosexuality is the cause of all suffering and one must therefore undo social norms, in many cases compounds the dissonance within homosexuals and their relationships, apart from creating havoc across social institutions. These concepts are developed in Chapters 3-4 in this book.

True compassion, as noted, balances judgment – a sense of boundaries – with kindness, in this case, respect for the heterosexual norm with love and care for the homosexual. This harmony of concerns is associated with beauty, for beauty is harmonization. One must, however, be wary of a corruption of compassion, which replaces this beauty, or harmony, of considerations of the other with a sense of one's own beauty in one's practice of seeming compassion. This can turn into a vainglory, which is imperious and intolerant of others. This narcissistic possibility of distorted compassion has become actualized in the contemporary culture of hedonistic materialism, which drives much of the same-sex marriage movement. Because it cannot bear any infraction of its own sense of personal beauty, its own regime of "compassion", it is particularly coercive when it comes to the freedoms of others. It closes down free discussion in academia and media; it seeks to invade and control religious schools; and it seeks to monitor and regiment the professions, pre-eminently psychology. Perhaps another reason for this coerciveness against freedoms may be its inkling that this dissolution of social boundaries leads to chaos, which can only be marshalled through repression. Not only, does its demolition of boundaries wrong and harm the family, the welfare of the homosexual him- or herself, and the education of children, as we wish to show, but it carries this all out fiercely.

The wrong against the family and its generations

The first area of wrong, coercively applied through homosexual marriage, is upon generations of unborn children. Since the human being uniquely knows him or herself as the offspring of its parents, homosexual marriage with its commitment to reproductive technologies with donor gametes and/or surrogacy creates generations of "orphans". In addition to this it delivers an instability into these marriages due to the same-polarity of the partners, with different generic forms of instability in male and female homosexual relationships. Moreover, the second-placement of children in same-sex marriage coheres with that of the defacto culture, in producing a general weakening of the family. Both are trends of the same thing. The outlook which places "love" and sex ahead of the interests of children is of a piece with the defacto culture, which does the same, by placing the cohabiting relationship ahead of a stable structure into which children are born. Both are symptoms of the culture of hedonistic materialism. These themes of the impact of homosexual marriage on children and the family are discussed in Chapter 3.

The wrong against the homosexual

Perhaps the profoundest victim of the ideology of same-sex marriage is the homosexual him- or herself. In reality, there is a wide spectrum of homosexual tendencies: from deep-seated predispositions through to less deep-seated tendencies which may have psychologically treatable causes, through to individuals who can and have had heterosexual relationships, but make a "lifestyle" choice to enter or experiment with a homosexual relationship. The attempted ban on reparative or conversion therapy tars all of these with one brush, where in fact – as documented by Robert Spitzer, Stanton Jones and others – therapy can and does work successfully for a significant range of the spectrum. The homosexual is locked in by the ban on therapy, his or her destiny sealed. The diversity of sources of homosexuality and its treatment, discussed in chapter 2, makes this "fate" imposed by the same-sex marriage movement the more poignant. The opposition of the psychological associations to therapy is no more than a corollary to the political – non-scientific – statement that homosexuality is a "normal" variety of human sexuality. In the United States this led to a travesty of justice in the refusal of a court, which shut down an agency offering this therapy, even to *hear* expert evidence of the success of reparative counselling.

The ban operates not only through peer-marshalling and threatened deregistration of professionals who offer counselling. It has emerged in legislation in Australia in the device of the Victorian Health Complaints Act of an inquisitorial Health Complaints Commissioner, who has been politically charged, with the assistance of third party informants, to search out and eradicate all such counselling. These themes are discussed in Chapter 4.

The wrong against education

The most concerning impact and coercion worked by the same-sex marriage movement is the attempt to educate young children in "sexual diversity". This posed originally as a movement to stop the bullying of homosexually inclined children, though it was clearly intended (as one of its designers admitted) to teach "sexual diversity" to young children. Whilst bullying of any kind and for any reason is cruel and must be stopped, the "Safe Schools Coalition" Program (with different names in different States) was introduced into schools primarily in order to win acceptance for homosexuality as a norm in childhood education, the best place to accomplish an overall cultural shift. The Labor Party, newly elected in Victoria in 2014, declared before its election an intention to impose this program on every Government School, which having been elected, it is now carrying out. The program invites young children to identify themselves sexually (heterosexual, homosexual etc) and thereby to lock themselves into a sexual identity. At an age where, according to some paediatric opinions, up to 26 per cent of children experience fluidity in their sexual identity, this is plainly dangerous. A girl's crush on another girl could be identified and confirmed as lesbianism. Quite apart from the ethical wrongness of this program, significant psychological harm could be imposed by presenting sexual options to young children for their selection and identification. The program not only uproots the moral culture of the Judeo-Christian or Abrahamic tradition, it also endangers children's normal development. This trend has been backed up in Victoria by three supplementary measures: (1) the exclusion of optional traditional religious education during school hours (and its replacement by a compulsory neutralizing and relativising comparative study of religions); (2) announced legislation to prevent religious schools from selecting staff who model the religious ethos of the school, where this conflicts with the "same-sex marriage" agenda; finally, (3) it has introduced a program into the school syllabus throughout the school years, to relativise religion as a comparative general study, in place of instruction of children in their actual beliefs. These themes are discussed at length in Chapter 5.

It is not only the education of children, which has been affected by the wider ideology of same sex marriage, hedonistic materialism, but also the very freedom of debate and enquiry in the Universities. One of the most disturbing features of the movement to institutionalize homosexuality is the intensity of the attempt made to silence reasoned and critical discussion of it. The ideology of "marriage equality" as part of hedonistic materialism is a credo of the politicized culture of the universities. From the universities come cadres of journalists, school teachers, bureaucrats, lawyers and health professionals all steeped in the same credo. From kindergarten to the University and its professional graduates, the coercive culture of hedonistic materialism corrupts education in the widest sense.

2

Homosexuality and the human being

Overview

Homosexuality is external to the *essential* human being – the soul or moral conscience, made in the image of G-d – which excludes it from its moral compass. The sources of homosexuality may operate on each of the levels of the human being, body, mind and soul, singly or severally. Each level indicates a different level of response.

In the bodily "somatic" dimension, a male's masculinity and a female's femininity may be weak, in terms of heterosexual attraction, due to temperamental or physiological factors, constituting predispositions to homosexuality. Where dissonance is experienced through the collision of these homosexual feelings with a social norm or personal norm of conscience the question is what medical and spiritual resources can be mustered to actualize or accommodate the moral norm.

In the mental or psychological dimension of homosexuality, it may be that trauma, abuse or developmental psychodynamics have subverted and inverted a normal movement into heterosexuality. Here the issue is how to employ counselling to recover lost heterosexual potential.

On the plane of, and against, spirit or soul, homosexuality can come about through a cultural "ethic" of homosexuality that supplants the soul and its commitments. Ordinary polymorphous perversity, latent in most people, is enough to fuel this "life-style" choice. The response to this cultural homosexuality is specifically through the language of the soul: to beam upon the soul the light (the "talk" and example) which revives its natural resonance with universal values and their sexual ethic.

The bodily dimension

Physicality and purpose

Whilst homosexuality may derive from a combination or variety of factors – physiological, psychological and cultural – in the following discussion each of these sources of homosexuality is considered in isolation. This is not so much a scientific exercise, as a philosophical comparison of the approaches of the Abrahamic faith tradition and hedonistic materialism to homosexuality on each of these levels. In separating out these levels I have sought to follow, according to my understanding, the methodology of Viktor Frankl's "dimensional ontology" of human psyche. Frankl would characteristically distinguish between the somatic or bodily, the mental or psychological and the existential or meaning-related manifestations of individual psychic conditions. Thus, for example, he sought to distinguish depression as an organic or somatic condition, a psychologically or mentally caused depression and an existential depression, such as depression due to a void of personal meaning. Depression can exist singly or severally on these levels, but an important task is to distinguish and identify the phenomena. The same applies to the levels at which homosexuality manifests itself.

The first of these levels is somatic. There is no conclusive theory of somatic (i.e. physiological) causes of homosexuality. There are a variety of suggested causes for the "inversion" of the normal sexual "object" – why a female seeks a female instead of a male and a male seeks a male instead of a female. There are theories which relate homosexuality to temperament and heredity, to intrauterine stress, sibling patterns, physiology of the brain and so forth.[1] Rather than attempt to evaluate or report evaluations of these different theories, let us instead address the moral and philosophical question: given, say, the presence of effeminate characteristics in a male or masculine characteristics (such as a "rough and tumble" predisposition) in a female, do these warrant their education and socialization into homosexuality? Or, if a person has grown into adulthood with sexually

---

1 See in general K.J. Zucker and S.J. Bradley, *Gender Identity Disorder and Psychosexual Problems in Children and Adolescents* (New York: Guilford Press, 1995) for a resume of theories of physiologically based homosexuality.

inverted interests, a male for a male, or female for a female, does this necessitate their expression in homosexual relationships?

Clearly, traditional culture has sought to socialize boys into a masculine role and girls into a female role, regardless of variations in temperament within each group. Its view is that the Creator has fashioned different kinds of physical persons and different species of creatures and entities within the Creation, each with broadly assigned purposes, which should not be confused with one another. And so too, sexual relationships between humans and animals are regarded as "confusion" of the distinct identity intended for each species. The Creator of the species has purposes for each of the species, defined by their physical characteristics.

Similarly, within the species of the human being, the physical characteristics of different genders relate to different, Divinely assigned tasks. A male human being is one with male genitalia and a female is one with female genitalia, and with this come distinct functions and moral obligations.[2] The Divine norm relating to human sexual unions is that a biological man should marry a biological woman and endeavour to form a family through which they procreate and produce further generations. Those who do not marry, for whatever reason, should not engage in homosexual relationships. The norm is expressed in the biblical verse, "So shall a man leave his father and mother and cleave to his wife [, from which is derived, not another man,] and they shall become one flesh [in their offspring]".[3]

Hedonistic materialism rejects the concept of a correlation of moral purposes and identities with the physical characteristics of humans and things. As expressed in the writings of Peter Singer[4], the principal exponent of hedonistic materialism (though he may not call it by this name), the human being is just another kind of animal and there is no Creator, Who assigns purpose and boundaries in the Creation. Beyond homosexuality, he

---

[2] A hermaphrodite (i.e. who has both male and female genitalia) is a distinct class with its own moral rules According to the tradition which has come down from Mt Sinai, a hermaphrodite is permitted to marry a woman, but a man is not permitted to marry a hermaphrodite. Surgery to "reassign" sexual gender is also not permitted.

[3] *Loc.cit.* Lesbianism is separately prohibited.

[4] Whose central ideas are expressed in *Animal Liberation*, New York: Ecco, 2002.

has also argued that bestiality is not immoral.[5] Every sentient being, in this theory, is entitled to pursue pleasure and enjoyment, crossing boundaries and altering moral identities, so long as it does not infringe the enjoyment of others.

In accordance with this principle, hedonistic materialism separates "sexuality" and "gender". It maintains that "sexuality" is what one physically is and "gender" is the sexual identity and role one would like to have. Instead of the Abrahamic faith tradition's notion that G-d has assigned delimited roles to all kinds and species, hedonistic materialism makes roles appropriable through desire. The latter view facilitates not only homosexuality, but also transgenderism, that a man may identify as a woman and a woman as a man, and beyond that to pursue transgender surgery to refashion the physical body in accordance with the desired sexual identity and role. This notion has moved now to the "gender-neutral" education and socialization of children in Sweden, suspending their gender identity until they choose it. In general, it is the desire of the psychophysical organism, not a moral obligation which devolves from the Creator (and personal conscience) upon the psychophysical organism, that determines its moral role and conduct. Whilst the expression "desire" is used, since it is the desire of the psychophysical organism, in fact this is not desire in the sense of "choice". To the contrary according to the standpoint of hedonistic materialism, the homosexual can be no other than what his or her physical "emergent characteristic" drives him or her to be. The disagreement between the Abrahamic and the hedonistic materialistic world-views has been put by the eminent psychologist Stanton Jones in these terms:

> [...V]arious religious views, especially the great religions of the book, Judaism and Christianity, and to a certain extent perhaps even Islam, believe that to be a human is to be in a sense in a conflicted situation. That means where and what we are is not necessarily what we're meant to be or called to be. This actually came out in a report from the American Psychological Association[6] in a very

---

5 Peter Singer, "Heavy Petting", *Nerve*, 2001.
6 American Psychological Association (2009). *Report of the APA Task Force on Appropriate*

profound way, where a group of gay activist researchers talked about the potential conflicts between psychological and religious views of a person. They talked about how the gay-affirming view – the psychological view – believes in what they call a sort of *organismic congruence*, that is, that a fundamental purpose of our human life is to embrace what we experience ourselves to be as defined by our instincts, by our biological urges. They contrasted that with what they called *telic congruence,* that is common in religious groups, coming from the Greek word *telos*, namely, the purpose or ultimate goal of our existence. I think they are pointing to something that is really true: that the great religions confront us with the fact that we are not what we're meant to be and we have to sort out what G-d's calling is; what the true calling of our humanness is – in our experience of this conflictedness. There is a sense in which the psychological and contemporary mental-health views are really minimizing this conflictedness and complexity of human existence. Years ago, the great Oxford don, C.S. Lewis, commented about the inadequacy of telling us to follow our instincts. He said, telling a person to follow his or her instincts is like telling a person simply to obey people. The problem is that different people say different things, so whom do you listen to? That is an existential human dilemma – which instinct do I listen to? It doesn't solve things to simply blunt our awareness of these broader existential questions. [...T]his [is the] question of how this reality that we are souls, and not reduced to our mere physical impulses, changes the formula for understanding who we are.[7]

The standpoint of the Abrahamic faith tradition is that a human being is a mixture of body-mind (the "psychophysical", to use Frankl's term) and soul. Very often these are in conflict. The psychophysical organism, with mind operating as the guardian and agent of physical impulse[8], seeks kinds of gratification, which the soul knows it is not right to pursue. There may be an impulse to steal, an impulse to hurt another physically, an

---

Therapeutic Responses to Sexual Orientation, p. 18; at http://www.apa.org/pi/lgbt/resources/therapeutic-response.pdf.
7 Stanton Jones and Shimon Cowen, "Psychology and the concept of the human being", *Journal of Judaism and Civilization*, Vol. 10, 2014.
8 Mind can also operate as the agent of the soul in mustering feeling (the body) to the imperatives of the soul or conscience.

illicit sexual impulse, which the soul, by reference to its Divine template, conscience, knows to be wrong and intervenes to check. Within the conflict of the psychophysical organism and the soul, there emerges freedom and responsibility to act or take up a stance. The highest self – the soul or conscience – has to arbitrate in that which the body wants: to evaluate whether the desired object is legitimate or not. Invoking its Divine, objective template of values, made articulate by religious tradition, conscience needs to be the ultimate authority within the human being.

Applied to homosexuality, this means that even in cases where that homosexual predisposition seems to be organic, to be part of the temperament of the physical being of the person, one still by reference to, and by strength of the spiritual faculty has to say "no" to the gratification of homosexual impulse. As discussed earlier, a paedophile may also have a deep-seated orientation, but this cannot be grounds to permit the indulgence of that orientation. The essential spiritual component within human can and must remain in charge. If one cannot do this by oneself, one should seek therapeutic and counselling to get the best possible outcome. Frankl stressed that the essential quality of the human being is the ability to transcend one's internal and external predicaments. Therapy should include this prompt to transcendence. For the religious person, the attempt to sanctify oneself, that is to say, to assert the soul's independence and "resistance" to all the pressures of one's physical being will be answered by G-d's help in doing so.[9] Against so deep-seated a desire a profound power must be invoked.

Dissonance

On the plane of somatically influenced homosexuality, some homosexuals experience "dissonance", subjective distress relating to their homosexual inclinations, which can lead to depression and even suicide. The source of the dissonance is a clash either with their own internal sense of what is right behaviour, an ideal which they feel unable to accomplish. Alternatively, (or

---

9 The highly successful "12 step" program of dealing with alcoholism also invokes a "higher power".

in addition) it can be dissonance with social values, with consequent social disapproval and rejection of that behaviour. Often personal conscience and social disapproval coincide, because they derive from the same moral code. Society, based on the values taught by the Abrahamic faith tradition, rejects homosexuality and so will the private conscience of the homosexual whose soul is consciously alive to that faith.

The reflex of hedonistic materialism to dissonance is to change the social and personal norm. Like Freud, who spoke of the socio-cultural "Superego" as bridling instinct and personal gratification, it sees social rejection (for which it has coined the term "homophobia") as the cause of unhappiness. Where there is no express social rejection, the suffering of the homosexual is put down exclusively to "internalized homophobia" – the homosexual wreaks society's "prejudice" against him- or herself. It goes further than Freud through the actual movement legislatively and administratively to deconstruct and deregulate society in a way which matches personal abnormality and to harass and punish those who uphold the traditional concept of normality. Happiness, it is claimed, will come when individuals are free to follow polymorphous impulse. The problem is, of course, that physical gratification does not equal happiness. To the contrary, behaviour is encouraged which is dissonant with the individual's (however latent) conscience and sense of wrong. The human being is driven by hedonistic materialism against his or her own essence into an existential void and crisis. Instead of releasing dissonance by permitting everything, hedonistic materialism can in fact compound it.

Freud himself understood very well that a major way in which the homosexual impulse in humans is checked and channelled into normal development is through society's public disapprobation of homosexual practice. Bullying and ostracism are coarse and reprehensible expressions of society's rejection of homosexuality and may compound the distress of the homosexual. But by the same token, to reverse the social norm and deconstruct it through encouraging "sexual diversity" does not solve the homosexual or society's problems. One removes the dissonance not by taking away conscience and moral social structures, but by helping to alleviate homosexuality. One needs to strengthen the norm, with sensitivity, both in society and as it is present latently or consciously in the conscience of the homosexual; and with appropriate medical assistance, love and care, help the homosexual deal with his or her feelings.

As noted, true compassion says, There is a boundary which one should not cross, but I feel for you and want to help you. It does not say, There are no boundaries. So society must eliminate bullying and acknowledge that this exacerbates suffering, without validating homosexual conduct. Professor Stanton Jones remarks further:

> With regard to [the] question about the causes of anxiety and depression and suicidal thoughts in homosexuals, I think the crucial thing is that the answer to the question is that is not either-or. It is very clearly not necessarily caused only by social rejection; nor is it due only to internal causes. The stress among homosexuals is just as complex as the stress among any population within human existence. The empirical evidence – a robust finding that comes out in every high quality studies – is that there are higher rates of a variety of forms of psychological stress and self destructive behaviour among populations of same-sex orientation. And you're absolutely right: if you accept homosexuality as a normal, acceptable condition as a presupposition, then you have to explain the distress by external factors and so there's a strong push to look at factors that may well be operative. (That is what many advocacy groups want to claim.) If I'm prone to depression or frustration or anxiety already and I'm persecuted for certain characteristics, that certainly will complicate my situation. So I don't think we can do away with that social stigma hypothesis as a contributor. I think the deeper question is whether it is necessarily the only cause.[10]

The response of hedonistic materialism is quite simply that the homosexual is "not broken" and does not have to be "fixed" and the *only* source of the homosexual's suffering is social rejection. But that is not the experience of many homosexuals in whom the soul is awake and who seek compassionate help, with whatever resources and treatments are available, to be what they know is right, to be their truest and deepest self. For those homosexuals whose homosexuality appears most "innate",

---

10 Jones and Cowen, *op. cit.*, p. 47.

that is, somatically influenced, the spiritual resource to be found in the identification of the essential spiritual "I", which can separate itself from their physically experienced homosexuality and take up a stance against – to change and modify – it, is of crucial significance. To withhold the help of the small G-d, the soul, and with it the great G-d, from homosexuals is to leave them with a virtually insurmountable obstacle in actualizing the fact that "predisposition is not predetermination".

The mental-psychological dimension

The psychological causation of homosexuality

In the foregoing section, we spoke of the source of homosexuality which may pose the greatest challenge for change. This is a predisposition of a bodily-based or temperamental homosexuality: a man has seemingly "innately" diminished sexual interest in women, and a woman in men. There appears to be a deficit in the very resources of masculinity and femininity in the "somatically" conditioned male and female homosexual respectively. The concept of psychologically caused homosexuality – conceptually isolated – is different. Here the individual *does* possess a good potential for arousal towards the opposite sex, but as a result of psychological developmental factors, this potential has been suppressed and inverted into homosexuality. Here one certainly cannot argue that the homosexual was "born that way".

Even physiological or temperamental factors cannot force a human being to act homosexually, so long as that person is aware of his or her own sovereign self, the soul, which acknowledges the heterosexual norm. It could be, that a man with an effeminate temperament and a woman with a more masculine temperament can galvanize masculinity and femininity out of their very beings with the will to embrace the spiritual norm. In the case, however, of mentally or neurotically caused homosexuality, the task of personal change and transformation is not confronted with as difficult a challenge.

A variety of factors can operate to produce homosexuality in a person who is temperamentally open to a heterosexual relationship. The following are examples of kinds of psycho-developmental problems or traumas, which have derailed an otherwise normal heterosexual development in a person. One is where a person in childhood has suffered from molestation by a person of the other sex. This may cause a child to retreat from heterosexual sexual intimacy. Sometimes it may arise from bad dynamics with persons of the same sex. A classic instance of this is rejection of a son by the father and abnormally high bonding with the mother. So also a sensitive boy may be rejected by his male peers, or a "tomboy" girl by her female peers. There may be familial dynamics, such as where in a bad marriage, a boy becomes the confidante and "surrogate husband" of his mother. Significant exposure to homosexual pornography may also play a role. Freud noticed that girls, who retain an infantile love for their parents beyond puberty "make cold wives and remain sexually anesthetic".[11]

The theme in psychologically developed forms of homosexuality is about waylaid or lost potentiality for heterosexuality. There are a variety of therapies available to help homosexuals recover their masculinity or femininity. Here is not the place to discuss these therapies, other than to note that they have helped many people, as discussed in Chapter 4. Hedonistic materialism does not acknowledge this and conflates all kinds of homosexuality, whether somatically or psychologically or even culturally based, into a category of immutable "born-that-way"-ness which cannot and should not be "fixed". In the case of one activist, whose own history contained extensive homosexual sexual molestation, this refusal to distinguish factors and any kind of treatment was expressed in the words, "I don't care how I became gay". All these words do, is to impose a "destiny" on oneself, which locks out freedom and responsibility. Precisely by understanding the sources and causes of one's homosexuality, does a person regain the possibility of bringing one's essential self to deal with that which is not one's essential self.

---

11 "Three Contributions to the Theory of Sex", Pt 1 "The Sexual Aberrations" in *The Basic Writings of Sigmund Freud* (transl. A. A. Brill), NY: Random House, 1938, p. 618.

The positive role of mind

Just as it is mind which in the case of psychologically influenced homosexuality has "inverted" sexual development, so it is mind which via various therapies can undo the inversion. The dogma of hedonistic materialism that all homosexuality is the same and cannot be changed, as little as can the colour of one's skin, is not only conceptually false; it is belied by actual experience.

Despite the figures documenting success in reparative therapy (see Chapter 4), to counter by saying that individuals have also failed in such therapy and as a result have become depressed or sought to harm themselves says nothing other than that those efforts failed. Is this is not true also of a wide variety of patients suffering from schizophrenia, bipolar disorder, depression and various anxieties, that their specific efforts and the therapies applied to them have on occasion failed, and as a result they fell into depression and even committed suicide? But did that fact invalidate the clinical effort of patient or therapist to work with schizophrenia, bipolar disorder, depression and various anxieties?

Even though psychologically caused – or neurotic – homosexuality is something which can be approached by retracing its personal history and re-mentoring the individual to his or her heterosexual potential, the spiritual dimension is required here too. For mind – notwithstanding its power over the development of feelings – can be fickle and bribed by impulse. It can be used to rationalize raw and unethical impulse, just as it can be invoked to review and check raw and unethical impulse. But mind has no moral anchor *in itself*. This is why even the psychological approach to the treatment of homosexuality needs to open the mind to the moral compass of the soul or conscience, made in the image of G-d.

In discussing the difference between (somatically or bodily influenced) psychosis and mentally influenced neurosis, Frankl makes this point, that neurotic conditions (including neurotically acquired homosexuality) must also be referred to the soul, as I have written elsewhere:

> [In Frankl's words,] "The human – and *precisely the neurotic* – has no greater need than to be as aware as possible of his or her own

responsibility." For if the psychotic – somatic – level of the person cannot *itself* listen to the highest self's (the soul's) presentation of meaning, the mental psychic level *can*. Frankl cites Ludwig Klages' description of *"Geist als Widersache der Seele"*, "the spirit as *counterweight* to the mental [the potentially neurotic] realm." Thus, P. Polak writes that logotherapy can help the patient to grasp neurosis as a possible but false "capability of being" (*Seinkönnen*), and cause "neurosis to be seen as the expression of a spiritual crisis." The patient is to grasp the opposition of the neurosis to his or her essential self. The compulsion, for example, which the neurotic experiences, must be comprehended by him as something "that he 'has', that is 'in him', but that is not 'he himself'. The neurotic must know him or herself as free to "accept or reject the promptings of impulse".[12]

In short, just as there is a greater freedom to change a psychologically than a somatically influenced homosexuality so there is also a greater responsibility to do so. But this in turn cannot be assured unless mind is referred to a higher faculty and source. For if mind is left unconnected to the sovereign realm of conscience it will end up the trustee and agent of mere desire, or some other fad of popular culture.

When mind opens to conscience, that is to say when it genuinely seeks self-transcendence, it affords the human being a truly objective, independent sense of self. The sense of the strength of conscience, that is not driven or determined by circumstances which impinge on the person from within or without, is the most powerful resource of the human being's ability to take the measures needed to deal with homosexuality or any other challenge. Mind comes into its full significance as that which connects feelings to values when it grasps itself as the conduit for values, which reside in the sovereign spiritual self to which it is beholden.

Hedonistic materialism, in its denial of the human soul and the Creator, which the soul mirrors, does great damage to the critical and reflective function of mind. As noted, what gives mind its power of critique, reflection

---

12 S. D. Cowen, "Viktor Frankl: Person, Philosopher and Therapist", *Journal of Judaism and Civilization*, Vol. 7 (2005), p. 19.

and review of feeling is its independence from feeling. Its independence is in turned guaranteed only by its ability to open to a naturally self-transcending faculty, the soul or conscience, which lifts mind into a relationship of detachment from feeling. If mind does not receive from a higher source, it becomes reduced to feeling, or little more than the cunning which helps desire obtain its objects. So in educational policy, hedonistic materialism, instead of allowing children to receive values from their parents who in turn draw on the collective conscience of millennial faith traditions, tell children to make up their "own minds" on moral questions. Of course, the syllabus, by which children are to discover their own ethical truths, is itself laced and led by the assumptions of hedonistic materialism and guided by *its* teachers. The most extreme form of this – which connects with our discussion – is the invitation to children to discover and posit their own sexual identity. At precisely the time, when identity, including sexual identity, is most fluid, most in need of education and socialization into normative moral conduct, hedonistic materialism encourages fluidity. They are taught to act out immediate and raw desire. This is the antithesis of an education and it robs the child of an ultimate, objectified sense of self, anchored in something other than impulse.

So hedonistic materialism has disabled the critical, reflective, exploring function of mind whether in the classroom or the university lecture room. It locks the door on therapy for the homosexual (as we shall see in chapter 4) the most poignant victim of the same-sex marriage ideology. It tells the homosexual, whether somatically or neurotically influenced, you *are* your desires, and any voice inside you to the contrary is simply "internalized homophobia". The schoolyard bully who assails the dignity of the child by conflating homosexuality with the child's essential personhood is more than matched by the bullying of hedonistic materialsm, which conflates the essential person of the same individual with – locking in – his or her homosexuality. Both bullies punish and deny human dignity, freedom and responsibility.

Cultural homosexuality

Homosexuality as an "existential" choice

Beyond the homosexuality which is predisposed by somatic conditions and that which derives from psychological and developmental origins, is an "existential" homosexuality. The somatic homosexuality may be the hardest to deal with. The neurotically conditioned homosexuality may be less so, because such individuals have a stronger capacity for heterosexual relations in their somatic constitution, but which has been developmentally derailed. By contrast, "existential" homosexuality is the "choice" of homosexuality, by people who may be somatically completely open to heterosexual relationships and free of psychological trauma, conducive of homosexuality. Rather, they have chosen to "experiment" with homosexuality or to embrace it as a life-style choice. Thus the man or woman who has raised a family in a normal heterosexual marriage, but now decides that they will now find "more fulfilment" in a homosexual relationship, has made an existential decision. It was possible, and perhaps even happily so, for them to live in a heterosexual relationship. It is possible now for them to live in a homosexual relationship because they have awoken the latent polymorphous perversity, which exists in most people, to drive it.

At a certain stage, homosexuality was culturally institutionalized in Greece, with men fashionably forming liaisons with boys *de rigeur*. This is a cultural homosexuality driven both by a philosophy which welcomed it and the human ability to find almost any impulse within him or herself. The world-view of hedonistic materialism also supplies the rationale for experimental life-style cultural homosexuality. It is a philosophy of the actualization of capacities for mutual "enjoyment", without any moral superior review.

This kind of cultural homosexuality, has a source in an idea expressed in a letter of Freud, who wrote to a potential client:

> I gather from your letter that your son is a homosexual. I am most impressed by the fact that you do not mention this term yourself in

your information about him. May I question you why you avoid it? Homosexuality is assuredly no advantage, but it is nothing to be ashamed of, no vice, no degradation; it cannot be classified as an illness; we consider it to be a variation of the sexual function, produced by a certain arrest of sexual development. Many highly respectable individuals of ancient and modern times have been homosexuals, several of the greatest men among them (Plato, Michelangelo, Leonardo da Vinci, etc).[13]

More recently a film about the great mathematician, Alan Turing, called "The Imitation Game", sought to make a similar point. Here was a homosexual whose genius in the development of computing helped significantly in the war against the Nazis to crack their secret military code and so shorten the war. The film's message is the injustice of any judgement of his homosexuality, (beyond his questionable treatment under the law of his times), *in view of his great achievement.*

The key point of this argument is essentially this. We see that individuals who have a homosexual lifestyle can function well. Not only this, they may produce contributions of genius. Additionally they may seem happy (though this may not be true of these cultural heroes). How then can homosexuality be regarded as an "illness" or "abnormality"? The answer to this is in understanding the distinction between culture (and science) and ethics.

Science, culture and ethics

Without question it is possible to have a disconnect between personal happiness and social functioning, on the one hand, and ethics on the other. Should psychology be concerned with that? If its sole tasks were to service personal happiness and social functioning, then a "well-adjusted homosexual" might not present as mentally ill. I do not think that psychology can suppress basic ethical issues, if for no other reason than that they tend to surface out of the depths of the human spiritual subconscious and create dissonance; and also because at some point fissures and dysfunction

---

13 This is part of the letter. For the rest see: http://www.lettersofnote.com/2009/10/homosexuality-is-nothing-to-be-ashamed.html

will arise in personalities, relationships and societies which operate against the ethical template prescribed by their Creator. If and when psychiatry and psychology do choose to become overtly concerned with ethical issues they will have to refer to sources outside themselves for the ethical principles with which the human soul resonates. We do, however, find that they make covert ethical judgments.

The statement issued by psychiatric and psychological associations that homosexuality is a "normal variety of human sexuality" is not a scientific statement. It is an ethical and a political judgment. The same will apply to pronouncements as to whether incest or bestiality are "normal": "normal" does not mean "it exists" and its practitioners are functional and happy; it means "it is co-normative". Indeed the gathering of the American Psychiatric society which declassified homosexuality as an illness, and has gone further to describe homosexuality as a "normal" variant of human sexuality was also driven by a political agenda of "gay rights", as accounts of the key 1973 meeting of the American Psychiatric Association, from a homosexual politically activist standpoint, openly acknowledge. Nevertheless, this non-scientific – covertly *political* – assertion of the American Psychiatric Association has spread throughout the world to give legitimacy, under the cloak of "science", to much harmful legislative and social engineering, oppression of personal and religious freedom and to the politicisation of justice (an example of which was the JONAH trial, discussed in Chapter 4).

Going back to Freud's letter, we could also ask, whether art and science necessarily go together with good personal ethics. If it is true, as Freud wrote, that Plato was a homosexual, is his philosophical system a reason to endorse his personal ethics? If Michelangelo and Leonardo da Vinci were homosexuals, does their art vindicate their (claimed) personal ethics? Alan Turing is one of the discoverers of the modern computer, which can (and was) used for great good, and can also be used for great bad. Does his discovery of a powerful technical instrument make his personal sexual conduct ethical? There is no logical reason to answer yes to any of these questions. Adding these names to enhance a culture of homosexuality, does not make it ethical or the cultural choice of homosexuality an ethical choice.

Exactly the false conflation of ethics with science and culture has enabled the cloak of the science of the premier American Psychiatric and Psychological associations to give validation to the political movement advancing homosexual marriage with all its appurtenances. In fact, their statement that homosexuality is a "normal variant" of human sexuality (and should not be treated) has no logical connection with the science of psychology, which indicates that under three percent of the population are homosexuals. "Normal" was a political statement and a cultural choice. The American Psychiatric and Psychological Associations are co-suppliers of the ideology of hedonistic materialism and cultural homosexuality.

3

Homosexuality and the family

Overview

Three aspects of marriage and family are negatively impacted by same-sex marriage. The first is the notion of marriage as the union of male and female, with their uniquely complementary qualities, modelling Divine or "cosmic" qualities, in their cofunctioning and providing role models to children. These are not available to the unit or children of a same-sex marriage. Moreover, there is a greater instability in the same-polarity of homosexual unions by contrast with stability of a complementary male-female union.

The second aspect of marriage impacted is its essential connection with the procreation of children and the provision of the required conditions of their nurture, development and care. Fundamental to this, is that children – as human beings – require identity. Central to human identity is the knowledge of, and relationship to, one's biological parents. Same-sex marriage cannot supply the full biological-spiritual nexus of identity between the generations.

Beyond the provision of identity for children, a third aspect of marriage is that it gives priority to a stable environment for the nurture of children and care of children. The significance of the formal legal commitment of spouses in marriage is intended no less for the children than for the "love" and sexual relationship of the parents. The impression that same-sex marriage puts "love and sex" ahead of children, as indicated by the systemic deprivation of the child's identity in same-sex marriage, is confirmed by a cultural correlation. Societies which have legalized same-sex marriage tend to have the highest out-of-wedlock birth rates: these are cultures in which "love" often comes ahead of children.

Man and woman

Masculinity and femininity as values

The biblical tradition speaks of man and woman as the partners to marriage. Marriage requires, but is not simply, the union of a man and woman. It is the formation of a home, into which children will hopefully be born and which will supply both the parents and their children's needs. That it biblically requires a man and a woman bespeaks a crucial concept of both the distinctness and the complementarity of masculinity and femininity in the family. Hedonistic materialism, on the other hand, attempts to deconstruct gender – traditionally male and female – into fluid, indeterminate and interchangeable identities. It tends to discard masculine and feminine as values, let alone require their complementary union in marriage.

"Masculine" is the quality, which it is a Divinely assigned task of the biological male, and "feminine" the quality, which it is a Divinely assigned task of the biological female, to develop with all their potentials. Through their opposite masculinity and femininity they are sexually drawn to one another to make procreation possible. Beyond that, other qualities are associated with male and female. Even though the roles may overlap in practice, and they carry with them no specific prescriptions for economic or social involvement, they have specific distinct roles for the formation of a home, in which children are raised. Generally, the father (male) is the more remote, abstract provider and the mother (female) is the closer, specific nurturer of the members of the household. To cite an ancient text, a man cannot be clothed by raw flax, nor nourished by a grain of wheat, though he can bring these home in considerable quantities. The woman, on the other hand, could convert the flax into linen and make from it garments to clothe a family; she could mill the wheat and make it into bread to feed the family. The same division of labour is replicated in sexual reproduction: the man provides the seed, the woman articulates, in the course of gestation, all the faculties and limbs of an entire human being. In general the male characteristic is associated with a more remote, abstract sustaining role whilst the female characteristic is associated with a closer, more specific, individualized nurturing role.

So too in the raising of children in the values of the home: in the father, a child sees the "colder" authority of values; in the mother it sees the "warmer" individualized application of those values. A child needs *both* of these masculine and feminine presences in his or her own upbringing; and in order also individually to model his masculinity and her femininity primarily on father and mother respectively.

Metaphorically speaking "masculine" and "feminine" powers, and their unification, are found also in the Divine. G-d has a transcendent "masculine" power, which constantly animates existence into being from nothingness. But G-d also has an immanent "feminine" power which "contracts" and differentiates that transcendent enlivening power into the vitality which is required to enliven each and every entity, according to its measure, in Creation. These two powers operate conjointly. Perhaps, part of the sense of the human being as made in the image of G-d, is that male and female join to create a child, just as G-d's transcendent ("male") and immanent ("female") powers operate continuously and conjointly to enliven and sustain the Creation.

Whilst it may happen that some men and women are physically unable to procreate through a physiological disorder (or because they are too old to do so), as genders they are suited to this purpose. Not only does the procreative union of husband and wife model a Divine concept. In reproduction the parents are also actually producing a Divine agency. Their purpose is to propagate not only physically (which is what animals also do), but also spiritually. This means that they extend themselves as a moral and spiritual agency through their children, who will actualize the ethical template of a Divine ethical code, recognized and imitated by the human soul, to do good in the world. One of the precepts of this code relates to legitimate sexual unions, specifically the heterosexual union which gives rise to marriage. A child needs to be educated by its parents to this universal value and to allow a child to be commissioned for a homosexual union is to teach it by example the opposite of what universal ethics prescribe in the realm of human sexuality.

Hedonistic materialism repudiates the concept of this Divine modelling and mission: instead of seeking to subordinate impulse to normative sexual identity, it wants to subordinate sexual identity to impulse. It knows of no objective morality, which parents should model, or children should learn.

The complementarity of the masculine and the feminine is a factor in the relative stability of the heterosexual over the homosexual relationship. Even where homosexual marriage has been legislated, as in Norway and Sweden, the statistics indicate a much higher rate of breakup in homosexual over heterosexual marriages. Charles Cook wrote in 2012:

> In Norway, male same-sex marriages are 50 percent more likely to end in divorce than heterosexual marriages, and female same-sex marriages are an astonishingly 167 percent more likely to be dissolved. In Sweden the divorce risk for male-male partnerships is 50 percent higher than for heterosexual marriages, and the divorce risk for female partnerships is nearly double that for men.[1]

Ostensibly there is deep-lying reason for this instability (aside from any personal factors in the individuals themselves). By raw nature the male, whose sexuality has a stronger genital component, as distinct from the female emotional and bonding element in sexuality, tends to promiscuity. Not only the anchor of conscience – the higher and truer self – can help a man restrain himself in this way, but also the anchor of his union with a woman. This is because a woman emotionally "domesticates" and "houses" a man, in a way that another man cannot. (This may have a Divine analogy in the way G-d's immanent power contracts and settles His transcendent power within the Creation.) Because male homosexuals are still male, though perhaps with a weakened masculinity, they are both temperamentally more "free agents". The anchoring of the inherently greater promiscuity in men is relatively weak in a male homosexual marriage. This leads to greater fracture of male same-sex marriages.

In lesbian marriages the same-polarity and non-complementarity produces its own form of instability. Amplifying the Norwegian and Swedish statistics, in the UK since the introduction of homosexual marriages the rate of dissolution of lesbian marriages is 3.2 times that of

---

1 Charles C. W. Cooke, "The Gay Divorcees", *National Review*, May 15, 2012.

male homosexual marriage dissolutions. The fact that the rate of divorce is much higher amongst lesbian than male homosexual marriages could be ascribed (as Cook does) to the trend that in heterosexual marriages more women are petitioners for divorce than men. In fact, however, the figures for the UK between 2011 and 2013 in heterosexual marriages were that the ratio of female to male petitioners for divorce was 2:1. This is significantly less than the ratio of 3.2:1 between female and male homosexual marriage dissolutions.[2] It does not disguise the high instability of lesbian marriage.

Beyond this, an exceptionally high incidence of domestic violence is cited in lesbian relationships. An explanation for this might be that just as the male-male non-complementarity works for instability so does the female-female non-complementarity. In that the feminine anchors, circumscribes and to a degree "possesses" the male, limiting his freer, more promiscuous tendencies, when two women live in the intensity of a sexual relationship, the possessiveness is compounded: the element of male detachment is not there to balance female possessiveness. Compounded promiscuity in male-male sexual relationships (whether married or unmarried) has contributed significantly to the devastating plague of AIDS; whilst compounded possessiveness in lesbian relationships accounts for the extraordinarily high level of violence and abuse found in them.

Children need mothers and fathers. Girls need a mother, who models femininity to them; boys a father who models masculinity. Both need both the complementary features of the more removed moral authority of the father and the close empathic, nurturing function provided by the mother. Where the masculinity of a male father or the femininity of a female mother is absent, children are deprived of the very role models needed to develop their own masculinity and femininity. This situation replicates to a degree some of the psychodynamic causes of homosexuality. And indeed same sex-couples are four times as likely to have homosexually inclined children.[3]

The Abrahamic faith tradition has understood that male and female

---

2 Figures from the United Kingdom Office for National Statistics cited in "Its women who want divorce, our study reveals", July 29, 2014 at http://www.justdivorce.co.uk
3 Stanton L. Jones, "Same Sex Science", *First Things*, February 2012.

and their complementarity, are the normative components of marriage. For this reason is it is important to foster masculinity, in its most wholesome form, and femininity in its most wholesome form in men and women respectively and to transmit this to the next generation of boys and girls.

Hedonistic materialism, on the other hand, as carried by the same-sex marriage movement is driven by its logic to "deconstruct" male and female gender. As noted, there is a movement in Sweden today to eliminate the distinction between boys and girls in schooling. Distinguishing male and female names, clothing and the toys traditionally specific psychologically to boys (trucks) and girls (dolls) are to be done away with. This has proceeded to the point, that a new neutral Swedish pronoun "het" is to be used in place both of "He" and "She". Children are not to be raised as boys or girls. It was also the first country in the world – in 1979 – to permit persons to reassign their gender ("transgender") through elective surgery. And in late 2015, the Swedish Government was considering implementing a report to allow 15 year-olds to undergo sex-change surgery without parental consent, and twelve-year-old's, who wanted it, with only one parent's consent (the Government being able to overrule the other parent if it thought it in the child's "best interest"). The dissolution of gender amongst children is the logical extension of the dissolution of gender amongst parents.

The family, children and identity

Marriage and the raising of children

The universal and enduring values, affirmed by the Abrahamic faith tradition, are ratified not only by the human soul but have also been transmitted through thousands of years of tradition. The former Chief Justice of the High Court of Australia, the Hon Murray Gleeson has spoken of how these universal laws or ethics should operate as background to the laws of society. He explains this in terms of the way the "positive laws", i.e. the laws enacted by societies and applied by judges are in fact *informed* by "universal laws".

... universal ethics *inform the content and the practical application of positive law*. In our positive law, whether it is judge-made law or statute law enacted by Parliament, there are many values from the tradition of universal ethics, that inform the law and are taken into account by judges when they interpret and apply the law... How do you tell the difference between a good law and a bad law except by appeal to some value or standard outside the law which you are judging? ... In conclusion, our positive law is suffused with values and principles that come from universal standards, universal ethics. And whether you find them in natural law, in Noahide law or more recently in declarations of universal human rights you are appealing to some standard outside the positive law.[4]

What this means is that there is standard outside and above the legislative and judicial activity of nations which civilization has ratified. A case of this is marriage itself. In the words of the Hon Murray Gleeson:

> The area of marriage provides a good example of the astonishing lack of reflection upon how and why [the law of marriage] got there. We have a definition in the Marriage Act which defines marriage as the union of a man and a woman to the exclusion of all others voluntarily entered into for life. Where does that come from? ...The Commonwealth Parliament in the Marriage Act has declared that marriage is an institution that needs to be *preserved and protected*. Again, where did that come from? Well, the answer, as a matter of history, is obvious. Until the nineteenth century, family law, the law of divorce and other aspects, was not administered by the ordinary Courts. It was the concern of ecclesiastic authorities, the Church court. That definition of marriage and recognition of marriage as an institution came into our law from Rome and it was the Church and the ecclesiastical courts which administered it. The Church took it from the Judaic tradition and the Judeo-Christian approach to marriage. [This] has entered into our law and is now described as an "institution" that needs to be preserved and protected. ...That seems to me to provide a textbook example of a value that has come into law from a universal value, and

---

4 "Ideals of a Justice System" *A forum with the Hon Murray Gleeson AC, former Chief Justice of the High Court of Australia in conversation with Rabbi Dr Shimon Cowen*, Melbourne: Institute for Judaism and Civilization, 2012. It appeared also in the Journal *Interface*, double biennial issue, Volumes 4-5, 2010-2014.

that has not been widely appreciated.[5]

The former Chief Justice goes on to specify that this concept of marriage – "the union of a man and a woman to the exclusion of all others voluntarily entered into for life" – is linked to the notion of reproduction, as a relationship of parents and children:

> The institution of marriage was not devised to cater for sex, but for the consequences of the procreative potential of sex. Specifically, it was a means of obliging males to take responsibility for their offspring. The family unit was considered the optimal environment for the care and nurture of children. If society is to sever, formally, the relationship between procreation and marriage, why should it retain the institution at all?[6]

The identity of children

The foundation of the raising of children within the family is a context of full and secure personal identity. The Bible's statement that "a man shall leave his father and mother and cleave to his wife and become one flesh" is explained to mean that man and woman become "one flesh" in the person of their offspring. Two people have become "one". This, which is possible only with a man and a woman, means that aside from forming their union with one another through marriage, they express their union outwardly through having children and creating a family. Biological reproduction creates a linkage between parents and children.

This has consequences for the identity the child. Just as the parents express their union through their offspring, so too does the child develop a unique and essential relationship to its parents. The child knows itself as the child of these parents. A commentator asks on the above quoted biblical verse "...and become one flesh...", is this not true also of animals? They mate and have offspring; they also become one flesh. What then is so special about a human child that he or she is uniquely referred to as the "one-flesh" expression of its parent's union? He answers that there is no

---

5 *Ibid.*
6 *Ibid.*

attribution of relationship between animals and their offspring: we do not refer to an animal as the "son [daughter] of so-and-so"[7]. Animals walk away and forget their offspring after the period of nurture, and so do the offspring forget their parents. With humans it is different: after the period of nurture is over, children continue to identify themselves as children of their parents, and parents as parents of their children. In other words the forging of parent-child identity is biological but more than biological. Other than to the breeder of the animals maybe, there is no interest in pedigree, no enduring subjective identity between generations of animals. For humans it is of enduring significance.

One reason why the lineage of generations is of subjective concern for humans alone is perhaps because human beings' reproduction is not only physical. The purpose of the human being is that he or she is a moral agent intended by the right exercise of free will to bring goodness – following a Divine ethical code, with which the soul resonates – into the world. When, as noted above, the human being propagates generations, he and she are also meant to be creating new agents of goodness. There is a continuity of mission and even more than this: the father and mother project their own spiritual identity through their children, even though it will gain the new individuality of their children's own personality and circumstances. Thus the individual has a spiritual history: a past – one's parents; a present, oneself and ultimately one's union with one's spouse; and a future, one's children. That is why education in values is so important: it has to do with the very spiritual continuity of the generations, manifested in the continuity and transmission of those values. *Human* biological genealogy is spiritual genealogy, and since essential self is spirit, therefore intergenerational identity is of great importance to human beings: these are my parents, these are my children. In a sense "they" are "I". For it is only the spiritual which travels on beyond the expiry of its bodily encasement. Even without an elaborate or even consciously religious sense, the human being intuits the centrality of parental identity. It is true that the lineage is important also for other matters, such as natural inheritance. But interestingly one of the deeper concepts of inheritance is that "the natural

---

7 The commentary *Gur Aryeh* of the Rabbi Yehuda Loewe (Maharal of Prague) on Genesis 2:24.

heir stands in the place of predecessor", that is to say, inherits *because* the heir is the extension of the predecessor.

This dimension of continuous biological spiritual identity is thus part of the human being's very makeup and can only be fully supplied by heterosexual marriage because the child knows and is raised by both its biological parents. In homosexual marriage, on the other hand, there is no one-flesh union in shared biological offspring. This means that the children must be "commissioned" by artificial reproductive technologies, through IVF with donor gametes or through surrogacy. The result is a child which is to be raised by "parents", one or both of whom are not his or her real parents. To adopt an orphan is a meritorious deed. To create orphans is not. But this is precisely what homosexual "marriage" does. Despite all the protestations of love, a human being is created with a deprivation of fundamental identity: to know and be raised by both of his or her parents. The fact that heterosexual marriages come apart and that children are brought up by a single parent does not take away the entitlement which in the first place should be granted to a child through heterosexual marriage: to know and be raised by its biological mother and father.

Of course, donor gametes are sometimes also accessed in a heterosexual marriage (where a father is infertile) and single women manage to access IVF with donor sperm. However, I once encountered a group entitled "Tangled Webs", who were born from donor gametes in the context of heterosexual marriages. They too shared a sense of deprived identity. Surrogacy carries the additional ambiguity, of whether the surrogate – birth – mother or the egg-provider is the real mother. But *all* homosexual unions sever an aspect of identity. No legislative fiat about who can name him or herself as a parent on a birth certificate can change the facts of identity. Even though suppression or confusion of biological identity is possible in some heterosexual marriages, it is inevitable in, and intrinsic to, homosexual unions.

The deprivation of generational identity is felt also by homosexuals. On one occasion at a forum, organized by my Institute, which broached, among other issues, same-sex marriage, a person stood up and identified himself as a homosexual and said: "I too want a mother and a father" – his own, natural parents, with the distinct qualities which each impart to a child's upbringing. Biological parents are also deprived, as Professor Patrick Parkinson has noted:

> One of the issues that has come up, quite often now, is homosexual men who donate their sperm to lesbian couples in order to help a woman in the partnership, have a baby and then they say, 'hey I want to see the kid, I want to be a father or uncle figure.' 'I want to see them regularly' or 'I want to be able to send birthday presents'. 'I want this child to know I am the father'. This has been the source of very considerable conflict and difficulty in the same sex relationship community.
>
> We've made an enormous mess of things by moving so far away from the foundational values, which have been formed not only by Judeo-Christian societies but by other societies around the world. We're now reaping the whirlwind that we have sown.[8]

Same-sex marriage and the breakdown of marriage

The artless formula of the same-sex marriage movement that "two people who love each other should be free to marry" is little tested or explored by those who use it. Its proponents in Australia have generally not considered whether it applies also to two adult siblings, who love each other. Sweden, which has thought the formula to its logical conclusion, does provide for incestuous marriage. But what is also unexplored in the formula is the "buzz" about "love" and its relationship to responsibility, especially responsibility to and for children. Prior to driving through legislation for same-sex marriage in Britain the British Prime Minister, David Cameron, said:

> [Same sex marriage is...] also about something else: commitment. Conservatives believe in the ties that bind us; that society is stronger when we make vows to each other and support each other. So I don't support gay marriage despite being a Conservative. I support

---

8 P. Parkinson and S.D. Cowen, "Family Law and the Biblical Concept of Marrige", *Interface*, (Double) Vols 4-5, 2011-14, p. 167.

gay marriage because I'm a Conservative.⁹

Have his words been borne out? We have already noted that the rate of breakup of homosexual marriages is significantly higher than heterosexual marriages. Additionally, however, the rate of homosexual marriage, where legalised, has steadily dropped in absolute terms, certainly in the instance quoted by Charles Cook:

> In the Netherlands, gay marriage is actually declining in popularity: 2,500 gay couples married in 2001 – the year it was legalized – and that number dropped to 1,800 in 2002, 1,200 in 2004 and 1,100 in 2005.[10]

The figures of higher break-up of, and declining entry into, homosexual marriage at one level belie the hopes of the British Prime Minister that homosexual marriage would foster a culture of commitment. But his hopes are false for a deeper reason. Marriage is an institution, set up, as he said, to create "bonds". Bonds, however, function when the parties to those bonds have natural relationships to one another, which the bonds reinforce. Since homosexual marriage is a part of a movement, which itself believes in the dissolution of natural relationships and boundaries, which puts love and desire ahead of them, what it does is to institutionalize the "institutionless". The figures quoted above speak for this.

The issue to be considered here is the relationship of "love" to responsibility for children. For this is what marriage is significantly about, in the words of the former Chief Justice of the High Court of Australia, quoted above, that marriage "was not devised to cater for sex, but for the consequences of the procreative potential of sex".

Despite all protestations of love for the children which have been "commissioned" through donor gametes and/or surrogacy for homosexual couples, the fact of the objective deprivation of identity to these children remains. Their "love" for the children is a love on the homosexual parents' terms, not the children's: their *ab initio* entitlement to full, natural identity and nurture with their biological parents was signed away before their creation was commissioned.

---

[9] Reported in the *The Guardian* (Australian Edition), 6 October, 2011.
[10] *Op. cit., loc. cit.*

There is another measure of whether a culture considers "love" between parents ahead of the needs of children, and this is in the culture of *de facto* cohabitation, where children are born outside wedlock. It is documented that children born outside the security of marriage are psychologically and educationally less well off[11]. Even though legislation has sought to impose mutual financial responsibilities on *de facto* couples comparable to that of marriage in the event of their breakup, this does not make cohabitation like marriage. For there has been no formal and legal commitment *from the outset*. On this, Professor Parkinson comments:

> ... there is pretty much no difference in law between being married and living together outside of marriage. The status of marriage – with its rights and obligations – devolves upon the *de facto* couple once they have lived together for more than 2 years, or if they have a baby; or alternatively (without either of these) if they register their relationship. Now, if by about two years of living together you are considered as if you are married you can imagine the shock that people feel when, through the practical effect of the legislation, they realize it. Many couples don't want to be married. They are testing it out, they are living together in case they might marry. They might marry someone one day, but at the moment they are just living together – no ties. Yet, in the law they are treated as if they are already married once they have been living together for two years...[12]

In other words, it makes no or little difference whether legislation makes a cohabiting relationship like marriage, if the couple does not enter into it with the intention of marriage, which is to establish an enduring union "voluntarily entered into for life." The figures bear out the weaker commitment and greater instability of *de facto* couples, especially as this impacts on children. In Kevin Andrews' words:

> In the US, parental separation by the time a child was age three has

---

11 See Kevin Andrews, *Maybe I Do,* Ballan: Connor Court, 2012, pp. 87ff.
12 "Marriage in contemporary Australian law" *Professor Patrick Parkinson in discussion with Rabbi Dr Shimon Cowen* in Rabbi Dr S. D. Cowen and Professor P Parkinson, "The biblical concept of marriage and contemporary family law in Australia", Melbourne: Institute for Judaism and Civilization, 2012.

been to be five times greater for children born to cohabiting rather than married parents. Two-thirds of children born to cohabiting parents will see their parents split up before they reach the age of ten (and three quarters by age of sixteen, compared to about one-third of children born to married parents).[13]

De facto relationships, into which children are borne, by definition have put "love" ahead of responsibility for children, because they have not created a framework which promises children the same stability and care for which marriage exists. This may well be due to cultural attitudes, which can be tested by looking at a comparable group of fairly prosperous and relatively culturally homogeneous countries in Western Europe. Here, we find that the top nine Western European Countries, in rates of birth outside marriage, have all legalized same-sex marriage. They are:

Country	Same-sex marriage	Ex-wedlock birthrate
Iceland	Yes	c. 65%
Norway	Yes	c. 55%
Sweden	Yes	c. 55%
France	Yes	c. 53%
Denmark	Yes	c. 45%
Great Britain	Yes	c. 45%
Belgium	Yes	c. 42%
Netherlands	Yes	c. 41%
Finland	Yes	c. 40%

Nine top Western European Countries by birth-rate out of wedlock (2011)[14]

In these relatively culturally and economically homogeneous countries high birth-rates outside formal and committed marriage coincide with legislated same-sex marriage. The societies which, in the words of the

---
13 *Op. cit.*, p. 88.
14 Source: OECD Family Database, OECD – Social Policy Division – Directorate of Employment, Labour and Social Affairs www.oecd.org/social/familydatabase

same-sex marriage movement, have put "love" first, making it the primary criterion for marriage, are those which put children second through a culture of *de facto* cohabitation with high out-of-wedlock birth rates. Homosexual marriage puts children second, because it deprives them of identity. So does a culture of *de facto* cohabitation, because it deprives children of stability. Both are symptomatic of a culture which puts "love" ahead of children. Whereas traditional marriage with a formally and legally committed mother and father and full bestowal of identity upon the child – insists that "love" be constrained by the highest responsibility for children.

The manoeuvring of a piece of legislation in the Parliament of the State of Victoria in 2008 showed the shoring up of a cohabitation culture in tandem with an attempt to replicate marriage for homosexuals. This occurred because Australian Federal law did (and does) not permit homosexual marriage and marriage under the Australian constitution is a Federal preserve.

The response of the Victorian State Government (which had an agenda sympathetic to same-sex marriage) to this fact at the time was to restructure the legal framework of cohabiting couples to make it almost identical to marriage. Thus, chunks of the Federal Marriage Act were taken out to apply to cohabiting couples who would enter their names on a Relationships Register. These couples could then access all the benefits of marriage (medical, pension, superannuation, tax concessions), as well as property division and partner and child support after breakup.

The intention of the State Government was that homosexual couples, who could not marry under Federal law (which governed marriage), would under this new State law, which was a "Relationships" Act, in fact enjoy all the benefits of marriage, without being formally married. The effect, however, seems to have been to boost the culture of cohabitation. Whilst couples would now be slugged with consequences (such as partner maintenance after breakup), that does not seem to have served to have made the entry into a cohabiting relationship any more conscious and committed in the first place, as Professor Parkinson has noted above. The consequences came as a shock to people who had drifted into a cohabiting relationship. But what the replication of all the benefits of marriage, for those without the commitment of marriage, did was to fortify the culture of non-commitment: "Why buy a cow, when you can get milk for free", as the vulgar adage goes. It made much more "milk" available, "without the purchase of the cow".

Those who were driving to provide an equivalent version of "marriage" for homosexuals, were at the same time bolstering cohabitation, the culture of non-commitment. The "love", which the same-sex marriage movement wants to make the supreme principle of a newly engineered concept of marriage, comes ahead of children. With this it strikes at the traditional concept of marriage, which links love to the best interests and deepest needs of children.

4

The same-sex marriage movement and the homosexual

Overview

It is a crucial axiom for hedonistic materialism that a human being is a driven organism, for whom choice against homosexual drives is not possible or at least not required. This chapter traces first the politics of the same-sex marriage movement within psychiatry and psychology, which now seeks political and legal means to block change for those homosexuals who do not want same-sex attraction. In fact this drive opposes the wishes even of those who argued for the declassification of homosexuality as an illness. The move to ban therapy negates the essential humanity and freedom of many (and potentially all) homosexuals.

Next, understanding the human as being essentially conflicted between impulse and conscience, body and soul, offers an understanding of the degrees of change of same-sex attraction, which are both possible and meaningful. It reveals that the comparison of homosexuality to skin colour and the proof criterion for therapy of total transformation of homosexual impulse or nothing, are both false. There is no absolute compulsion to homosexual activity and degrees of change are possible.

Finally, this chapter reviews some instances of the actual political and legal measures which impact not only of homosexuals but on religious freedom in general, wrought by the move to ban therapy for change. One was the JONAH case in the United States. The second is a new law of the Parliament of Victoria, Australia, to create a virtually unfettered Health Complaints Commissioner, politically intended to destroy reparative therapy. From the corruption of psychology, we have proceeded to the abrogation of patient autonomy and religious freedom.

The move to ban reparative therapy

Hedonistic materialism grasps the human being as an essentially material organism with a capacity for pleasure, which it is driven to maximize. It does not admit into the human being a soul, which can review and reject some of those impulses as inconsistent with the will of its Creator. The consequence of this single-dimensional view of the human being is that freedom and responsibility, born from and summoned by the conflict between impulse and conscience, does not exist for hedonistic materialism. The human being *is* his or her impulse and must pursue it like a purely animal or biological organism. From this comes the axiom, that homosexual attraction cannot be changed and that no effort should be made to change it. Only when the fulfillment of those drives could affect another, who is not able legally to consent, can there be a requirement that those drives be blocked. But a spiritual template which detects wrongdoing even in the context of consent, does not provide that justification for hedonistic materialism. Consequently, hedonistic materialism requires that therapy should not be available, whether for adults (who "mistakenly" want it) or for children, in the care of their parents.

In 1973 a major upheaval occurred within the American Psychiatric Association (APA), which resulted in a vote to remove homosexuality as an illness from the professionally "iconic" *Diagnostic Statistical Manual of Mental Disorders* ("DSM"). The accounts of this "revolution" cannot and do not disguise the fact that the revolution was over a view of what the human being "is". The APA overturned the Judeo-Christian or Abrahamic model of the human being, which biblically described homosexuality as a deviation in human behavior by reference to a spiritual-ethical norm and moral purpose or "telos" for the human being. The vote replaced it with what, as noted, has since been described as an "organismic" view of the human being, in which purportedly materially emergent characteristics state what the person "is."[1] The difference between these world-views has already been elaborated a number of times in this book.

Significant research carried out by the psychologist Evelyn Hooker in the 1950s was invoked to support the paradigm shift. She had studied

---

1 The terms here used are those cited by Professor Stanton Jones, quoted earlier.

personal histories of homosexuals, who did not suffer personal distress or social dysfunction – the customary markers of illness – through their homosexuality.[2] She did find some homosexuals with these problems, but these she ascribed to social victimization, not to factors such as personal inner dissonance.

The notion that homosexuality has no endogenous (inwardly caused) features of illness, but that illness experienced through it is exogenously (externally) caused through stigma and victimization fitted neatly with a hedonistic and materialist world-view. In this world-view, homosexual practice became an expression of human actualization. The American Psychological Association in 1975 followed the delisting of homosexuality as an illness by the American Psychiatric Association and this position became iron psychological professional etiquette throughout the western world including the Australian Psychological Society. The British Royal College of Psychiatrists tucked this into an overt political platform on matters normally debated and some not even considered debatable by legislatures. Before the introduction of homosexual marriage in the United Kingdom, the British RCP apart from requiring rights for homosexuals to form civil unions and to adoption and reproductive technology, also required religious orders (which would include Judaism, Christianity and Islam) to ordain homosexually practising ministers.

A recent "Report of the American Psychological Association Task Force on Appropriate Therapeutic Responses to Sexual Orientation" (2009) treats religion a little more gingerly. Whilst formally acknowledging that psychology should not interfere with the personal religious beliefs of patients, it would still not countenance therapy for a religious person wanting to modify homosexual inclinations in accordance with his or her religious beliefs. Instead it proposed that religious homosexuals look for elements in their own religious communities which would support and destigmatize their homosexuality; but it did not validate the personal religious reality of a person desiring to modify it or the position of those faiths themselves.

---

2 See below comments on the particular subculture of homosexuals which Hooker used for her survey.

Let us return to the "DSM-V" category of paedophilic disorder. It is one of a set of paraphilic (atypical sexual) disorders, which can be so classified if *either* (a) such individuals "feel personal distress about their interest, not merely distress resulting from society's disapproval" *or* (b) it is a "sexual desire or behaviour that involves another person's psychological distress, injury, or death, or a desire for sexual behaviours involving unwilling persons or persons unable to give legal consent". In other words, even if *subjectively* the individual disposed towards pedophilia feels no distress, the DSM was willing to call it a pathology if *objectively* it constitutes a moral, social wrong. The possible wrong, involved in paedophilia was that it could wrong "persons unwilling to give legal consent", that is to say, children.

Now with regard to this second, objective criterion of mental disorder, homosexuality stays out of the DSM, as a sexual disorder, because it operates within consent. But were it to be regarded as wrong, homosexuality (like pedophilia) would also be a disorder *whether or not an individual felt distress* on account of it. As noted, the materialistic-hedonistic "organismic" view of the person considers harm between persons as the only place of wrong. The Abrahamic world-view understands not only wrongs between persons, but also wrongs between persons and G-d, which since they breach personal identity are harmful to the person him- or herself. Homosexuality is in *this* category and moreover can be a source of experienced distress for those who have some degree of consciousness or intuition of their inner spiritual-normative identity, with which homosexuality conflicts. We have discussed the connection of heterosexuality, and disconnection of homosexuality, with this identity in Chapter 3.

The will and assistance to embrace a personal norm

In the decades following the 1973 resolution, the dominant culture in psychiatry and psychology went on to place a professional ban on reparative therapy for all homosexuals including those *subjectively* distressed by their condition. Beyond the intimidation – and implicit threat of deregistration and loss of livelihood – of dissenting therapists through the psychological associations, legal and political sanctions have been brought against therapy of this kind, as we shall later discuss in this chapter.

Professor Robert Spitzer, an eminent psychiatrist, was amongst those who "spearheaded" the removal of homosexuality as a mental disorder from the DSM in 1973. At the same time, he fought to retain as a category of disorder, "ego-dystonic homosexuality": namely the condition of one *distressed* by his or own homosexuality. Official psychiatry and psychology was now pressing on to fortify its stance on the normality of homosexuality by removing "ego-dystonic homosexuality" from the DSM and deeming therapies to change homosexual orientation as "unethical".

A colleague related to me in a personal communication that some time after the 1973 resolution, Spitzer spoke to him that about the result of a new study he had made. He had interviewed significant numbers of homosexuals, who entered programs to alter their sexual orientation, and now Spitzer observed that change was possible. He wanted to "repent" – presumably from the corollary of the APA's stance that since homosexuality was a "normal" form of human sexuality, that therapy to change it was misplaced and unethical. In his new paper[3], published in 2003, he stated the following conclusion:

> These findings of considerable benefits and no obvious harms in the study sample suggest that the current recommendation by the American Psychiatric Association (2000) that "ethical practitioners refrain from attempts to change individuals sexual orientation" is based on a double standard: It implies that it is unethical for a clinician to provide reparative therapy because there is inadequate scientific evidence of effectiveness, whereas it assumes that it is ethical to provide gay affirmative therapy for which there is also no rigorous scientific evidence of effectiveness and for which, like reparative therapy, there are reports and testimonials of harm.

Predictably, upon the publication of this paper, Spitzer faced an onslaught by the political wing of "gay psychology" attacking the study for its clear implications. Amongst the criticisms brought against him was that his sample of interviewees was supplied largely by an organization

---

3 "Can Some Gay Men and Lesbians Change Their Sexual Orientation? 200 Participants Reporting a Change from Homosexual to Heterosexual Orientation", *Archives of Sexual Behavior*, Vol. 32, No. 5, October 2003, pp. 403-417.

(NARTH) which helped *religious* homosexuals attempt to modify their sexual homosexual orientation. Had he drawn on a wider sample, it was argued, he would not have found a comparable rate of success in conversion- or reparative therapy.

But that is just the point. The relative success found in Spitzer's sample of *religiously motivated* subjects disclosed a dimension of human personality, which a materialistic and reductionist psychology could not find. The religious dimension in the lives of these respondents meant that *physical* impulses did not constitute the ultimate basis of their personal identity. Rather they recognized a tension between physical impulse and a higher self, with its normative orientation against this particular impulse. They were *distressed* by the dissonance between impulse and a spiritually perceived and ratified norm positioned against that impulse and were *motivated* to do something about it. Evelyn Hooker's sample of "happy and functional" homosexuals, recruited by the early radical gay rights movement, the Mattachine Society[4], presumably ideologically inured against religious consciousness, had yielded the opposite result.

Professor Stanton Jones reports similar experience:

> I and a colleague published a seven year outcome study looking at individuals who had undertaken sexual orientation change. These individuals had been involved in various Christian ministries. The study was published in a mainstream peer reviewed journal. Our study has been dismissed because we didn't do it on a "random" population. This is just one of many trumped up "methodological" charges that are posed against this exercise. I had to laugh at their objection, because if forced to compose a random sample, you will in fact be composing a sample of people who largely have been convinced by a culture, which has told them that there is no need or valid motivation for change and that it is repressive to try to change. It is only in a traditionally religious context that individuals come to the experience of struggle which gives them sufficient motivation even to attempt what can be an arduous process....Normal human experience is conflicted, it's complex

---

[4] As by noted by Thomas Landess in his study "The Evelyn Hooker study and the Normalization of Homosexuality" in the December 1997 NARTH Bulletin.

and it's difficult, but that's our human calling.

The furore from the "gay lobby", and the American Psychiatric and Psychological Associations which had absorbed its ideology, impacted on Spitzer. Already elderly and unwell (with Parkinson's disease and "battle-weary" from the controversy), Spitzer was drawn into various apologies. In a video interview, he stated that he regretted the political use made of his study by a group espousing traditional values, "Focus on the Family"; in a letter he expressed equivocations about his methodology. But with all these pressures, he still would not exclude the possibility of change for a homosexual seeking it. That is to say, he never repudiated his findings.

Professors Stanton Jones and Mark Yarhouse, in a study of homosexual participants in a Christian psychotherapeutic program "Exodus", published in 2011, found that "one third of the final participants abandoned their attempt to change, with many embracing a homosexual identity. About one third embraced sexual abstinence rather than a homosexual identity. About one fourth had moved away from a predominantly homosexual orientation and reported having satisfactory heterosexual relationships".[5] What this shows is that movements away *from* homosexuality and some *towards* heterosexuality are possible and documentably without harm. In all, *more than half* had changed.

---

5 Stanton L. Jones and Mark A. Yarhouse "Honest sex science", *First Things* (October, 2012), reporting on their study "A longitudinal Study of Attempted Religiously-Mediated Sexual Orientation Change", *Journal of Sex and Marital Therapy*, 37:404-427 (2011).

The meaning and scope of change

The spectrum of change

As discussed in Chapter 2, there are various bases for homosexuality: somatic, psychological and existential or cultural. It might be that the degree of "difficulty" in change corresponds with the causes influencing homosexuality. In some, it may be a more deep-seated "original" or "innate" (though that does not mean predetermining) homosexual predisposition, that could be related to a particular hormonal imbalance in the body or other physical factors. In others psychological developmental factors are stronger. Viktor Frankl made a clear distinction between the two, each requiring different kinds of intervention and offering differing prospects.[6] And Freud similarly distinguished the different types.

Specific clinical issues and causes are not the concern of this Chapter. Rather our concern here is to understand the degrees of success in therapy bringing a homosexual person to be able to function in accordance with conscience and consciousness of a heterosexual norm. The human being, as a mixture of body, mind and soul, necessarily has constant challenges from impulse, which are at variance with conscience. In spiritual and ethical terms, no person is to be "judged" for the *presence of* contrary or immoral thoughts and impulses, but rather on whether one (dwells upon them and) actualizes them in unethical conduct. Accordingly, the transformation of impulse and the "elimination" of homosexual fantasies may not be even a spiritual marker of success in therapy. The ability to function heterosexually is one measure of success. So too, the ability to contain homosexual impulse is another measure of success, even if that person cannot yet function heterosexually. This is the significance of the study by Jones and Yarhouse which saw a significant number move away *from* homosexuality and another significant bracket move *towards* heterosexuality. The idea that a person is healthy only when he or she has eliminated all conflict could in fact be the sign of a deeper pathology, as Professor Jones states:

---

6 Viktor E. Frankl, *Die Psychotharapie in der Praxis*, Wein: Franz Deuticke, 1947, pp. 61-73.

...There's been a lot of discussion in psychological and mental health fields for a long time on the idea that the simple absence of conflict doesn't mean the person is healthy. In fact the absence of conflict is diagnostic of deep mental illness often, for instance, in the psychopath or sociopath, in a person who inflicts cruel treatment on others but is unruffled about this. You don't say this person is marvelous and healthy because they can do these awful things and not feel conflicted about it. In fact you say it's problematic. So we need to grapple with how these existential dimensions - these moral dimensions of living - have to be factored into our judgments about what kind of health state we are in.[7]

Where inner conflict has been totally eliminated, we have either a psychopath or, in a *healthy* way, we have a saintly human being. For most people, from a religious point of view – one which acknowledges the presence of both body and soul – conflict is part of life and it is a question of managing, not eliminating our impulses. Professor Jones comments:

...I know a number of people who have made very significant changes, but the change is not like switching a light switch from pure homosexual to pure heterosexual.

There was a recent controversy here in the United States. The leader of Exodus International, which is a religious ministries group, an important group concerned with reparative therapy, was quoted as saying that of the majority of people he knew to be homosexual, 99.9% have not experienced change in their orientation. This quote was taken out of context and there was a lot of hooting and celebrating in gay advocacy groups as though he had said that change is actually impossible. Well, that does not actually state the whole of what he said. This 99.9% is made up of people who either haven't experienced change in their orientation or they have not gotten to a place where they can say they were never tempted, or they have not gotten to a place where they were tempted in some way. In other words, he was saying that if you think of sexual orientation as a continuum, there are a lot of people

---

7 *Op. cit., loc. cit.*

who have experienced movement along that continuum and have moved from being more homosexual to more heterosexual, but that doesn't mean that they never experienced any homosexual attraction. And I know from my discussions with this leader, Alan Chambers, that he does not say that he never experiences any homosexual feelings, but he has made significant movement. He is married, they adopted children and I've seen him and spent time together with him and his wife and they have a loving, caring close relationship.[8]

The goal of partial transformation

As noted, to achieve a total transformation of unwanted homosexual impulses and fantasies – namely that these should not ever occur to a person, even though they are not translated into action – is a very elevated goal: it is found only amongst the great. Even the psychologically and religiously "healthy" are not masters of all their thoughts. What they may be masters of, is not meditating on undesirable impulses and fantasies, and certainly not translating them into action.

Thus, where physiological factors incline a person to homosexuality, and means of treatment are not presently available, it is perhaps an unrealistic goal to expect reparative therapy to eliminate all homosexual fantasy and to have a high rate of movement towards heterosexual functioning. Where, on the other hand, homosexual impulses emerge in a person, who is in fact somatically unhindered in heterosexual relationships, but whose homosexuality has psychological sources, there might be more prospect of transformation towards heterosexuality, as Jones and Yarhouse found.

Interestingly, in Spitzer's 2001 study, cited above, whilst some of those who had been through therapy, continued after it to have fantasies of a homosexual character etc, what fell off almost totally were actual homosexual acts. In short the fact that one is also capable of heterosexual acts, is an indication of significant partial transformation of impulse. That some homosexual fantasies persisted is immaterial in terms of this accomplishment.

---

8 *Ibid.*

The limited objective of celibacy

There is furthermore the goal of celibacy for those homosexuals who find that they cannot function sexually with one of the opposite sex. This may be a sad and difficult situation, but it can be considered in religious terms a great achievement, given that person's personal challenges. For since in traditional religious terms, a homosexual act is a transgression, the fact that an individual was able to control him or herself in difficult personal circumstances is remarkable. Professor Jones speaks of such a case:

> There's a homosexual man that I've been friends with for ages in my community and he is someone who has sought out change, pursued change and for him change has been absolutely not forthcoming. Despite his best efforts to modify his experience, he has not experienced much change over these many years and he has maintained a chaste moral existence in accord with his religious beliefs during this time. Still, in terms of being capable of significant experience of heterosexual feeling that has simply not been his experience. So I think that sometimes despite all the goodwill and high motivation, change may sometimes not be possible.[9]

In spiritual terms, a great achievement occurred. The inner impulse may not have been modified. But that it did not carry into action, where once it did, is a *great* change.

In summary, the extraordinary achievement of the total transformation of impulse and fantasy, the partial transformation of impulse and fantasy into a working heterosexual life-style, and the turning away from homosexual activity, even if heterosexual attraction cannot be aroused, are all levels of achievement, to be respected according to the specific challenges facing each individual.

---

9 *Ibid.*

Faces of coercion:
the legal and political closure of patient autonomy

Around the world the same-sex marriage movement has sought by political and legal means to prohibit therapy for those seeking help from unwanted same-sex attraction, or who seek it for their children. It is portrayed as not only impossible but harmful. This is a mantra repeated vociferously by politicians and media, who have no critical understanding of psychology or the actual data. More disturbingly, it is repeated by professional psychological and psychiatric associations, which *do* have access to the data. The "Report of the American Psychological Association Task Force on Appropriate Therapeutic Responses to Sexual Orientation" (2009) was prepared by a committee of seven psychologists. I am informed[10] that politics went into the composition of this committee: of the seven members, six were homosexuals and therapists and one was a heterosexual but gay-affirming therapist – hardly a scientifically balanced panel. Notwithstanding this the conclusion of the Report, concerning purported harm arising from reparative therapy, was as follows:

> There are no rigorously scientific studies of recent SOCE [Sexual Orientation Change Efforts] that would enable us to make a definitive statement about whether recent SOCE is safe or harmful and for whom.[11]

Nevertheless the twin political (non-scientific) statements of professional psychological associations – (a) that homosexuality is a "normal" variant of sexuality and (b) that it is unethical to treat it – have formed the basis for legal and political persecution of homosexuals and parents wanting, and therapists willing to facilitate, change. Two examples are the JONAH trial verdict in the USA in 2015 and the Health Complaints Act passed by the Parliament of Victoria, Australia, in 2016.

---

10 By one psychologist who sought to be included in the committee.
11 Page 83 of the Report.

The JONAH trial

A Jewish organization set up to assist Jews seeking help with unwanted same-sex attraction (Jews Offering New Alternatives for Healing) was fined and ordered to close down by a New Jersey Court in 2015 on the grounds of "consumer fraud". The case was brought against JONAH by a "gay activist" organization, The Southern Poverty Law Centre, which found disgruntled individuals willing to be its plaintiffs. The charge was consumer fraud, namely that JONAH could not deliver what it offered, help to those seeking change with their unwanted same-sex attraction. The turning point of the case was the Judge's acceptance of the plaintiff's argument that JONAH's expert witnesses, licensed therapists, who were ready to testify about their success in helping individuals alter their homosexuality, should be barred from testifying. The Judge excluded the expert testimony *a priori* and out of hand on the basis of the cited pronouncements of the American Psychiatric and Psychological Associations that homosexuality was a "normal" variety of human sexuality and that therapy should not be undertaken to modify it. A case which was being heard on "consumer fraud", that the therapy did not work, would not hear testimony that it had worked. Early in the trial, Nicholas A. Cummings, a former President of the American Psychological Association (who himself had supported the declassification of homosexuality as an illness) made this statement:

> The Southern Poverty Law Center has done amazing service for our nation in fighting prejudice. But it has gone astray in its recent New Jersey lawsuit charging JONAH, formerly Jews Offering New Alternatives for Healing, a group that offers to help gay people change their orientation, with committing consumer fraud. The sweeping allegation that such treatment must be a fraud because homosexual orientation can't be changed is damaging. The lawsuit is the opening salvo of a wave of activism intended to discredit therapy offered in 70 clinics across 20 states, according to the SPLC.
>
> When I was chief psychologist for Kaiser Permanente from 1959 to 1979, San Francisco's gay and lesbian population burgeoned. I personally saw more than 2,000 patients with same-

sex attraction, and my staff saw thousands more. We worked hard to develop approaches to meeting the needs of these patients.... Of the patients I oversaw who sought to change their orientation, hundreds were successful.

I believe that our rate of success with reorientation was relatively high because we were selective in recommending therapeutic change efforts only to those who identified themselves as highly motivated and were clinically assessed as having a high probability of success.

Since then, the role of psychotherapy in sexual orientation change efforts has been politicized. Gay and lesbian rights activists appear to be convincing the public that homosexuality is one identical inherited characteristic. To my dismay, some in the organized mental health community seem to agree, including the American Psychological Association, though I don't believe that view is supported by scientific evidence.

...[C]ontending that all same-sex attraction is immutable is a distortion of reality. Attempting to characterize all sexual reorientation therapy as "unethical" violates patient choice and gives an outside party a veto over patients' goals for their own treatment. A political agenda shouldn't prevent gays and lesbians who desire to change from making their own decisions.

Whatever the situation at an individual clinic, accusing professionals from across the country who provide treatment for fully informed persons seeking to change their sexual orientation of perpetrating a fraud serves only to stigmatize the professional and shame the patient.[12]

In purely professional terms, this was a closure of patient autonomy – a wrongdoing. On a broader scale, it was not only a wrong-doing, but brought a punishment for doing right.

---

[12] Nicholas A. Cummings, "Southern Poverty Law Center wrongly fighting against patients' right to choose". *USA Today*, July 30, 2013.

The Victorian Health Complaints Act

On Thursday 25 February 2016 a bill was passed by the Legislative Assembly of the Victorian Parliament without even going to a vote. Yet there was something very disturbing about this bill, that not even members of the Opposition picked up. The bill has since become law, after passing the Upper House, the Legislative Council, where both major parties supported it. In the following I would like to highlight its disturbing features, which seem to have escaped – or been ignored by – many members of the Parliament, the media and (as a result) the public. It may have escaped scrutiny because it is cloaked in a noble cause: to help the vulnerable against medical frauds by a proactive intervention which scans the society and culture for health service fraudsters and initiates action against them on behalf of actual or potential victims.

The first problem, however, in this bill is its prime political intention. This is what the Health Minister in the most emotive part of her speech introducing the second reading of the bill, described as the bill's intention to eliminate the "abhorrent" practice of therapy for same-sex attraction. During the debate also this motivation was repeatedly referenced by the most vehement supporters of the Bill in both Houses of Parliament. The fact is, however, that *this* issue was a matter for debate, but received no debate in the Parliament other than reiteration of the mantras of the unethical practice of change for people who are "born that way". The JONAH case was also cited, as vindication for the eradication of reparative therapy, without any knowledge of how that case had been decided. At all events, to achieve this goal (amongst others) a super-commissioner who could be assisted by interested third party informers, was created by this Act to seek out and punish those who offered reparative therapy (amongst other "frauds").

Under the preceding legislation, it was the job of the Health Complaints Commissioner simply to respond to the complaints of victims. The new Act allowed the Commissioner to initiate the complaints as to what *he or she* finds unacceptable. The new bill also allows third party informants to initiate complaints as to what *they* find unacceptable. The complaint did not need to be confirmed by the individual, such as one seeking reparative therapy. The old law limited the Commissioner to complaints against practitioners from registered health services (doctors, psychologists etc). The new Act enabled the Commissioner to scan the entire culture for anyone offering health advice and take action (in this case to search out and "stamp out" reparative therapy by anyone offering it in any form). The new Act further accorded the Commissioner new punitive powers to issue interim and ongoing prohibitions against the provision of a health service and to name the service publically – without any open process or remedy. In this way a practitioner of reparative therapy could be faced with real destruction of a psychological practice and livelihood. In short, the new commissioner with his or her third party – in the case of reparative therapy, highly motivated – helpers and informants would know better than the patient what is good or bad for him or her and disallow it.

The creation of a super Health Complaints Commissioner with a potential legion of third party informant-helpers to find and prohibit therapists who offer help to those with unwanted same-sex attraction (because the patient him- or herself would not complain) has major consequences not only for ethics but also for democracy and human rights. First of all it gave the Commissioner super-legislative and judicial powers. The question of whether or not therapy for sexual orientation should be offered, is, as we have discussed throughout this book, one involving human values. There are a great many people, who on the grounds of conscience and religious belief, want to struggle with a whole variety of impulses, and do so successfully with or without therapy. It is not for an individual Commissioner to decide matters of conscience and values of individuals. Accordingly "bans" on reparative therapy, as it is sometimes called, in ordinary democratic theory, should be a matter for a public and parliamentary debate. The disturbing novelty of this bill was that its prime political intention – the "stamping out" of reparative therapy – was not made the subject of a political debate. Reparative therapy has been accepted or rejected in other parts of the worlds by *parliaments and courts*, not left to a commissioner, who is to be appointed with the intention of dealing with it outside parliamentary and judicial view.

In the US, there are four states which have legislated a ban, and sixteen which have rejected such a ban. *But it went to Parliaments, not to the discretion of a Commissioner.* Moreover, the four out of twenty American states which accepted the ban, that was proposed to them, did so only for minors. The other sixteen upheld, ostensibly that parents have a right to educate their children, which includes also supervising their physical and mental wellbeing The intention announced by the Minister for Health of Victoria that the Commissioner would uproot all therapy for unwanted same-sex attraction made no distinction between minors and adults. But usurpation of a political and legislative role by the newly envisaged Commissioner could hurt many more than those seeking help with unwanted same-sex attraction. The health sphere is full of issues with political dimensions, be it abortion, euthanasia and palliative care and many others. Let all give thought to what they wouldn't want a Commissioner with personal prejudices – uninstructed by Parliament or public debate – to allow or prohibit.

Beyond this, the search-and-punish function of the new Commissioner with his or her voluntary third party helpers could cause a lot of other harms.[13] Yet all of this was purchased through a principal motivation to eliminate reparative therapy. It illustrates how the opposition of hedonistic materialism to a religious world-view ends up by damaging the best of democracy and suppressing open debate. In these legal and political actions, the first victim of the same-sex marriage ideology is the homosexual, who wants to actualize what is experienced as his or her deepest ethical self; the second, the therapist who would help; and the last is the rest of us.

---

13 The example has been suggested to me of the ex-spouse of a health practitioner who wants to get at the practitioner for purported malpractice towards another. And what about the privacy of a supposed victim, on behalf of whom a third party wants complain, when the Commissioner responds to that third party's complainant with private information about the victim?
 The capacity of the Commissioner to cause harm, with new punitive powers accorded him or her, constitute also an unscrutinized judicial power. Under the Act, the Commissioner can place an interim *and* ongoing prohibition on a practitioner and name the practitioner publically with potential destruction of the practitioner's livelihood. Where is the openness of the "judicial" process which led to this harmful ban and naming, and what is the remedy for the practitioner for lost livelihood, if it is successfully appealed? Where does the public see or know if the Commissioner is making his or her own essentially political decision on a health practice (like therapy for unwanted same-sex attraction), where there is no legislation or judicial precedent?

5

The same-sex marriage movement and the education of children

Overview

Integral to the ideology of historical materialism and its program of same-sex marriage is an attempt to change the culture at its root: in the education of children, the next generation. In its programs of teaching "sexual diversity" in schools, under the ruse of countering bullying, is first of all an attempt to dissolve the nexus of values between parents and their children. This is aimed at stopping the transmission of values in the Abrahamic faith tradition and in the process violates a number of principles of religious freedom.

The second strategy of the same-sex marriage movement in education is to cultivate a cultural homosexuality in children, by suggesting alternative identities to them at the stage of their greatest fluidity of identity and activating homosexual potentials which could otherwise largely be socialized into heterosexuality. The ruse of anti-bullying has since been admitted by a leader of this movement: the real goal was the teaching (and propagation) of "sexual diversity".

The third aspect of the educational program of this arm of hedonistic materialism is actually to intervene against religious education in schools, to cancel religious instruction not imparted in the home. It has done this politically in Victoria by driving Special Religious Instruction out of school hours in Government schools; and by proposing to interfere in the staffing of private, religious schools; and also by introducing a new syllabus into all schools, both Government and private (including faith-based schools) which relativizes and "neutralizes" religion as a comparative "general" study, not one of personal belief.

The dissolution of family and parental influence

It is a long established principle of the ideological reconditioning of a new generation, that the education of children must be severed from parental influence. It was standard practice in the totalitarian regimes both of Nazism and Communism. The deepest source of transmission of values in the Abrahamic faith tradition is the home. However attenuated religious practice may have become, some 70 percent of Australians still profess a religious affiliation and values are passed on from generation to generation in the home. If parents today are weak in their transmission of values, they can at least remember what they learnt from *their* parents.

It is this residual memory of transmitted values, and the basic faith underpinnings which go with it, which produces the outrage when parents find that their children are being exposed to explicit "sexual diversity" in new programs of the same-sex marriage movement such as the "Safe Schools" program, which has gained significant traction throughout many schools in Australia. It made inroads through compassion for its professed goal, to stop the bullying of homosexually inclined children. This ruse, as has since been (unwittingly) conceded in a video, in which a leader of the program acknowledges that:

> Safe Schools Coalition is about supporting gender and sexual diversity. Not about celebrating diversity. Not about stopping bullying. It's about gender and sexual diversity.[1]

It offers a smorgasbord of sexual identities to children and seeks to create an environment in which sexual diversity is "celebrated". This movement has proceeded to the point where it received not only State but Federal Funding, until a recent outcry lead to a national review of the program.

The "audit", put out by the Safe Schools Coalition Victoria, seeks to determine whether a school is "safe" against homosexual bullying, asks whether "diverse sexualities" are "celebrated" by the school, in its library collection, teaching curriculum and so on. Here, as part of its program, it requires schools to teach ("celebrate") the acceptability of homosexual

---
[1] https://www.youtube.com/watch?v=j5uNocBCw3Q&feature=youtu.be

behaviour as a norm. By so doing, it flies in the face of over 3000 years of religious and cultural tradition since Sinai, the tradition of most parents of school children. In terms of the traditional world religions and world civilization, it is teaching something which is a moral wrong and fundamentally unethical. Here, of course, the world religions will acknowledge a full distinction between the person and the behaviour. The precept of love of another *person* applies under all circumstances whether to the heterosexual or to the homosexual.

Moreover, to introduce acceptance of a "norm" of homosexual behavior under the rubric of "tolerance" is false. Tolerance has to do, as Viktor Frankl said, with love and respect for *people*, not for their views or behaviours. It does not extend to a moral relativism which makes the unethical ethical.

The movement constitutes a significant attack on religious freedom. It seeks to interfere actively with the values transmitted through generations of families – something for which a State educational system has no permission. Certainly no permission can be found from the doctrine of the separation of religion and state in the Australian and American constitutions. The relevant parts of both constitutions (section 116 of the Australian constitution and the first amendment of the US Constitution) provides that the Government shall not *establish* a religion, but equally that it shall not *exclude* religion. It does not mean that religious values are prohibited expression in the public sphere. To the contrary, the State is recipient of values which well up from a broad public, and if these values have a religious character, the State is bound to reflect them in its public policy. Constitutional doctrine affirms religious freedom. To filter and reject religious values is a restriction of religious liberty which the Australian Constitution in section 116 itself upholds. Private institutions may more wholly reflect the values of their specific constituencies. The "battle" of ideas and values is in the public square. Where generally the public square has a religious character, this may be reflected as they are in the prayers with which Parliament begins. This is not strange in a society in which 70% of the population, according to the last census, identify with a traditional religion. Notwithstanding this, individuals are not compelled to participate in the prayers.

Even though the Federal Constitution in section 116 does not address the States but only the legislative activity of the Commonwealth in the realm of religion, its principle of the free practice of religion is of deep significance for all Australian society. The program set out by the Safe Schools Coalition is an assault on religious freedom: the freedom of parents to have their children educated in their religious traditions, or at least *not* to have these traditions and their ethical principles *negated*. Yet this program seeks to do so by imposing on educational policy a world-view or ideology, which is essentially hostile to traditional religion and its values.

The doctrine of hedonistic materialism, with its acceptance of homosexual practice as an ethical norm, is a political and cultural movement which seeks to override the great world religions. According to the spirit of freedom of religion in the Constitution therefore, it should *not* be allowed this dominance. Nevertheless, the homosexual anti-bullying program requires a school to teach *every* child in the school acceptance of homosexual practice as co-normative with heterosexual practice. The approach is identical to the stratagem of "hate crime legislation". Legislation and the courts, must, according to proposals for "hate crime legislation", enshrine the principle, that a crime committed with the extra factor of animosity towards homosexuality must incur an *additional* penalty, to teach society that homosexual behaviour is an element of the dignity and integrity of the human being. The "right" to homosexual practice thereby becomes encoded as a universal principle on a par with equality of all persons, regardless of race. The problem here is that civilization endorses the equality of all humans in that they are all made in the image of G-d, with the same spiritual potentiality. It does not endorse homosexual behaviour; but a sleight of hand, a cultural, political and educational maneuver, is trying to sanctify it.

The homosexual school program seeks coercively to impose its world-view – including its teachings concerning homosexuality - on an entire school population. The notion that *all children* in a school (of which a great many come from religious backgrounds which prohibit homosexual behavior) must be taught in the school from infancy that homosexual behaviour is equally normative, is coercive. State institutions – state schools – are being required by it to teach values, which infringe religious liberty. Proposed American congressional legislation of exactly the same kind, "The Safe Schools Improvement Act", comes with a threat to withhold state funding from schools in which bullying of homosexually disposed children occurs, with the implicit requirement that the school must teach the acceptability of homosexual behaviour to meet the grade and receive continued funding.

Not only does this practice of inculcating a specific norm into all students, not authorized by the public or reflecting its differentiated make up, violate the spirit of religious freedom exemplified by the Constitution. It is also a violation of international rights as set up in instruments of the United Nations. Specifically it is in violation of the UN Convention on the Rights of the Child which in article 14 states:

> **Article 14**
> 1. States Parties shall respect the right of the child to freedom of thought, conscience and religion.
> 2. States Parties shall respect the rights and duties of the parents and, when applicable, legal guardians, to provide direction to the child in the exercise of his or her right in a manner consistent with the evolving capacities of the child.
> 3. Freedom to manifest one's religion or beliefs may be subject only to such limitations as are prescribed by law and are necessary to protect public safety, order, health or morals, or the fundamental rights and freedoms of others.

The homosexual anti-bullying school program, with its indoctrination of the "normativity" of homosexual practice from early child education violates every one of these articles, which entitles a child coming from a home in which religious belief prohibits homosexual behaviour, to preserve that belief.[2] The right to that belief in no way clashes with "fundamental rights and freedoms of others": it does not have to be abandoned in order to stop bullying, as the Safe Schools Coalition, spuriously and by its own acknowledgment *tactically* claimed, as we shall now discuss.

---

2 See also the Victorian Charter of Human Rights and Responsibilities, section 19 (1) which affirms the right of every individual to "practise his or her religion".

The ruse and intent of the educational program

Setting aside the unethical and disenfranchising aspects of the program, there are several grounds on which the actual methodology of the project to stop bullying of children manifesting homosexual inclinations is either misguided or generative of fresh harm. These have to do with (1) the question of psychological validity of the program to combat bullying (2) the appeal to children to identify and confirm their sexual orientation and (3) the very focus of the program on sexuality and sexual behaviour of children itself.

Ms Evelyn Field is one of Australia's and possibly also internationally one of the primary experts on dealing with bullying in schools (and other contexts). She has written books on the subject and also has a website (bullying.com.au). On a radio program, which I hosted, she stated that the method of dealing with bullying of any kind is not to engage the issue which is the pretext for the bullying. If a child is being bullied because he or she is obese, there is no need to engage the bully or the school environment with a discussion of obesity, let alone to extol it. You don't stop the bullying of a fat child by celebrating obesity. She stated that the way to stop bullying is to block it by showing the bully that you are not upset. You don't get angry, you don't walk away. You neutralize it by indicating that whatever you say is not going to distress me, so don't waste your time. The methodology is not to engage in the issue for which the bully is bullying not to get involved in the pretext or the subject of the bullying. If one teaches a child how to "block" a bully it doesn't matter what the bully is saying or attacking, the same response applies.

In a nutshell, if a child is being bullied because he or she is fat, the way to block the bully is to take the "wind out of his or her sails", it is not necessarily to take up the pretext upon which the child is being bullied. By extrapolation from Ms Field's words, if a child were being bullied because he or she had stolen items, the purpose would also not necessarily be to take up the issue of theft. Bullying is something which is independent of the "cause" in which it is pursued. It is reprehensible in and of *itself*. It might be added that children can bully out of cruel and vindictive grounds.

They could also bully out of morally defensible grounds – such as taunting a child who had a pattern of theft. The taunting and the bullying would be wrong. The grounds might have a moral content. Our civilization of thousands of years does not regard homosexual practice as normative, but as a moral wrong. The opposition to homosexual behaviour and the revulsion experienced against it has a moral basis. Violence, taunting and bullying has no moral basis. This further brings out the point, that the issue over which the bullying occurs is not relevant to the very act of bullying, and the attempt to connect the two can backfire on the blocking of bullying. It could wrongly be used to "justify" the bullying of a child who (and *because* he or she) steals.

However, the homosexual anti-bullying program, having violated this methodological principle, goes on to create circumstances of actual harm. By calling on children to identify themselves sexually at young age (to lock themselves into a sexual identity in early or pre-adolescence), they seize upon an as yet fluid and unformed sexual identity. There are cases where peer groups have labelled a child as homosexual, and the child has taken on the identity, only to cast it off later amidst much suffering and much bad experience, when the child finally socializes into a normative heterosexual role. However, here it is not peers but social workers and academics who are working to freeze a child into a sexual identity – an explicitly homosexual identity at a young age. The *New York Times* with its program of adolescents "coming out", publicizes the manifestoes of young children about their supposed homosexuality. The active acculturation of children – in an extremely fluid stage of their personal identity – into homosexuality is a profoundly disreputable professional practice. Evelyn Field states: "I don't like the idea of locking a young child into anything at a young age. We know that children are not developed intellectually until their mid to late twenties (or is it late teens to mid twenties?). We know that when they are at school they are still confused as to who they are and how they fit in with their peers and society. We know that they are physically developing. We have a cocktail of hormones which means that the young person is really insecure as to who they are and who they will become."

The effect of this program is to *cultivate* homosexuality within a wide range of children who in the course of time and with the support of traditional values, could readily emerge from identity-uncertainty into traditional heterosexual roles. The American College of Pediatricians[3] (quoted below) notes that up to 26 per cent of young children have sexual identity uncertainty. Under 3% of the adult population have settled into homosexual practices. This means that the homosexual school program potentially works to encourage the remaining 23 to 24% to the position that homosexual life styles are an acceptable option. The present program, working upon the fluid sexual identity of children, can only be to cultivate and extend homosexual conduct amongst many children who would otherwise be socialized into normal heterosexual conduct.

There is finally the question of why there should be so much talk about sexuality in a curriculum, whether hetero- or homosexuality. Is this not itself an incitement or encouragement to sexual activity at an age at which it is wholly inappropriate? This is a highly sexualized society. No kind of sexual activity should be suggested or encouraged at the onset of puberty and adolescence. The present program is a contribution to the hyper-sexualization of society, starting with children. This is morally wrong; it is ostensibly bad for children's own development and it can lead to pregnancies and feeds into a culture of abortion. It detaches moral responsibility and commitment from sexuality, since children at this age are clearly incapable and are not legally permitted to form committed relationships. It essentially pressures children into sexuality at an age where they are not psychologically or even legally ready for it. It teaches sexual activity outside maturity and commitment. In short it is a driver to promiscuity, which has in certain countries taken the form of "educating" children in explicit homosexual

---

3 The American College of Pediatricians distanced itself from the American Academy of Pediatricians (AAP), being founded by a past president of the AAP. It is based consciously on a different ethic and model of the human being from that of the AAP. The AAP has an allegiance to the teaching of the American Psychiatric Association in its new ruling about the human being in 1973. Essentially, it would appear that the American College of Pediatricians hold to the traditional view of the person as body and soul, in the context of objective and eternal norms, which sees the "basic father-mother family unit, within the context of marriage, to be the optimal setting for childhood development, but pledge[s] our support to all children, regardless of their circumstances". On the other hand the AAP subscribes essentially to a materialistic perspective on the human being, in which the spiritual within the human being is held to possess neither truth nor objectivity, and the human being is essentially driven by a material complex of impulses.

devices and practices.

No legitimacy can be extended to this program "professionally" by the fact that university departments are involved with the program. University faculties and individual academics have ideological commitments like anyone else. Thus I heard the decision to continue the homosexual anti-bullying program of the "Safe School Coalition Victoria"'s work and its continued funding is up to its evaluation by Latrobe University's Department of Education and Early Childhood Development. How can a body which is in partnership with the Safe School Coalition Victoria, and which itself ostensibly benefits from the same funding be expected to provide an objective analysis? The "evaluation" must come also from bodies, which do not have the university's financial and ideological pre-commitments.

The "science" and statistics of the program

In Victoria, a Minister of an earlier Government was moved to fund the trialing of Safe Schools Coalition Victoria program, through persuasion of an MP who was reported in the Parliamentary record, *Hansard*, to have said:

> I implore the minister to look at the figures on youth suicide and self-harm and to recognise that these kids struggling with sexual identity are overrepresented in these statistics. A staggering 25 per cent of 15-to-24-year-old gay and lesbian kids have suicidal thoughts, and 80 per cent of bullying behaviour of gay and lesbian kids occurs in schools.

The prompts here to introduce the "Safe Schools" program are (a) the incidence (though this is unspecified) of bullying of homosexually inclined children (b) the presence of suicidal thoughts in children with homosexual tendencies and (c) the imputed association of bullying with the suicidal thoughts.

Whilst fully condemning the bullying of any child whether on grounds of obesity or homosexual behaviours or any other reason, let us look at the statement made in Parliament. First *no* absolute figures of bullying of homosexually inclined children are given. Undoubtedly there are some, but no absolute numbers are given, on the basis of which a universal program is mooted to teach the normativity of homosexual practice is schools. The same question arises in the comparable stratagem to introduce extra penalties for assaults on homosexuals under proposed "hate-crime" augmented penalties. What are the absolute figures of the instance? Again this will not be to exonerate or deny actual instances of violence, but we need to know the extent of the phenomenon for which such global "remedies" are proposed.

Secondly, the 25 per cent of homosexual persons with suicidal thoughts quoted refers to "kids between the ages of 15 to 24". Within this bracket the only years relevant to a school population are the ages 15 to 18, and we are not told what percentage of this bracket have suicidal thoughts. Moreover the school program is also geared to children who are well beneath the age of 15. They may not have suicidal thoughts but they are, under the program, subjected to intensive homosexual acculturation programs.

The third and most important question on the statistics is *why* do these children or young adults, with sexual identity confusion or homosexual leanings, have suicidal thoughts? Is it (solely) because of bullying or because of the essential malaise of confused identity? The President of the American College of Pediatricians has written:

> Bullying has been linked to various negative outcomes among students; however, a direct link to suicide is less clear. Suicide most often occurs as a culmination of long term internal struggle and unrest. It is an irrational act of desperation that is often associated with the presence of long standing mental illness, depression, substance abuse, and isolation in its victims. More than 90% of adolescent suicide victims met criteria for a psychiatric disorder before their death. Even suicide victim advocates caution the media against portraying bullying as the "cause" of suicide, stating that it ignores "the underlying mental illness issues that are present in 90% of the people who die by suicide." Some advocates for those expressing alternate sexual identities also caution against the claim "that bullying caused someone to die by suicide." Their concern is

that by oversimplifying an association, individuals sympathetic to a cause or group may commit copycat acts of suicide.

Again, to point out that 80% of bullying of homosexuals goes on at schools does not contribute to the argument. Presumably 80% of bullying on all accounts and for all sorts of pretexts goes on at school. But if bullying is not the primary determinant of suicidal thoughts, then the "80%" cannot be grounds to propel a global program of affirmation of homosexual practice in schools.

A fundamental tenet of the "science" of the same-sex marriage movement is that all homosexuality is "hardwired" into a segment of the population. From a religious standpoint, if a person felt an overwhelming homosexual impulse of the deepest nature, that would be viewed with compassion but it would not constitute permission to indulge homosexual activity in practice, however deep the inclination. We have discussed this at length. It is an abnormality, which, as far as possible, should be treated. But there is also a wide spectrum of children and persons who experience sexual identity confusion (including homosexual impulse) and can yet prevail upon themselves to accept what for the world religious cultures is the normative model of heterosexual behaviour. The same-sex marriage lobby has a stake in rejecting both therapy and the idea that many humans can change and/or take control of their impulses. Paradoxically, it can be argued, their attempt to block this change and drive children deeper into malaise is the potential cause of great suffering. Those who insist that a child *is* homosexual and *should* embrace a homosexual lifestyle can compound the psychological malaise. Indeed it has been reported to me that many formerly homosexual people say that "they considered suicide *because* they had been persuaded that they had no hope of change". The following is a letter from the President of the American College of Pediatricians, Tom Benton, to American School Superintendents on March 31, 2010:

> Dear School Superintendent,
>
> The American College of Pediatricians shares with you, your staff, parents, and other professional organizations the common goal of providing a healthful environment for your students. We are increasingly concerned, however, that in many cases efforts

to help students who exhibit same-sex attractions and/or gender confusion are based on incomplete or inaccurate information...

Adolescence is a time of upheaval and impermanence. Adolescents experience confusion about many things, including sexual orientation and gender identity, and they are particularly vulnerable to environmental influences.

Rigorous studies demonstrate that most adolescents who initially experience same-sex attraction, or are sexually confused, no longer experience such attractions by age 25. In one study, as many as 26% of 12-year-olds reported being uncertain of their sexual orientation yet only 2-3% of adults actually identify themselves as homosexual. Therefore, the majority of sexually-questioning youth ultimately adopt a heterosexual identity.

Even children with Gender Identity Disorder (when a child desires to be the opposite sex) will typically lose this desire by puberty, if the behavior is not reinforced. Researchers Zucker and Bradley, also maintain that when parents or others allow or encourage a child to behave and be treated as the opposite sex, the confusion is reinforced and the child is conditioned for a life of unnecessary pain and suffering. Even when motivated by noble intentions, schools can ironically play a detrimental role if they reinforce this disorder.

In dealing with adolescents experiencing same-sex attraction, it is essential to understand there is no scientific evidence that an individual is born "gay" or "transgender." Instead, the best available research points to multiple factors – primarily social and familial – that predispose children and adolescents to homosexual attraction and/or gender confusion. It is also critical to understand that these conditions can respond well to therapy. Dr. Francis Collins, former Director of the Genome Project, has stated that while homosexuality may be genetically influenced, it is "… not hardwired by DNA, and that whatever genes are involved represent predispositions, not predeterminations." He also states [that] "…the prominent role[s] of individual free will choices [has] a profound effect on us." The National Association for Research and Therapy of Homosexuality (NARTH) recently released a landmark survey and analysis of 125 years of scientific studies and clinical experience dealing with homosexuality. This report, *What Research Shows*, draws three major conclusions: (1) individuals with unwanted same sex attraction often can be successfully treated; (2) there is no undue risk to patients from embarking on such therapy and (3), as a group, homosexuals experience significantly higher levels of mental and physical health problems compared to heterosexuals.

Among adolescents who claim a "gay" identity, the health risks include higher rates of sexually transmitted infections, alcoholism, substance abuse, anxiety, depression and suicide. Encouragingly, the longer students delay self-labelling as "gay," the less likely they are to experience these health risks. In fact, for each year an adolescent delays, the risk of suicide alone decreases by 20%.

In light of these facts, it is clear that when well-intentioned but misinformed school personnel encourage students to "come out as gay" and be "affirmed," there is a serious risk of erroneously labelling students (who may merely be experiencing transient sexual confusion and/or engaging in sexual experimentation). Premature labelling may lead some adolescents into homosexual behaviours that they otherwise would not pursue.

Optimal health and respect for all students will only be achieved by first respecting the rights of students and parents to accurate information and to self-determination. It is the school's legitimate role to provide a safe environment for respectful self-expression for all students. It is not the school's role to diagnose and attempt to treat any student's medical condition, and certainly not a school's role to "affirm" a student's perceived personal sexual orientation.

From the natural fluidity of sexual identity, which arouses doubts in the minds of 26% of 12 year old children, but yet settles statistically to under 3% of adults, we see the profound danger in the attempt to persuade children of a supposed homosexual identity. Not only this, it is the persuasion to identify as homosexual which arguably *increases* suicidal thoughts. The child is being driven by this program against its most natural identity.

The suggestion here is that the freezing of young children into homosexual identity may be a much greater factor contributing to depression and suicidal thoughts than bullying. The bullying must be stopped, but to use the bullying as a pretext to intensify the confusion or disorder is unconscionable. Secondly, and conversely, this movement closes the door on therapy. The difference between 26% and under 3% indicates that therapy, where needed, could help out of identity confusion 23% of those 26%. There are educational systems, running with the homosexual program, in the world which encourage transgender identity in children of kindergarten age. How will this *enlarge* the present 26% of gender confusion in 12 year-olds before the next step is taken to confirm them into non-heterosexual practice?

The "science" behind the homosexual program for children in schools has gone beyond the ideological overthrow in the American Psychiatric Association in 1973, which declassified homosexuality as an abnormality. It seeks now to "grow" homosexuality from early childhood, to make homosexuality a central feature of contemporary culture.

The closure of religious education in schools

It is one thing to introduce a program into schools which contradicts the parental and familial transmission of values and another to gear this to children at the most fluid state of the formation of their own identities. But still there might remain in schools sources of religious education – not from parents – but from teachers from religious orders, who could yet impart the values, including the sexual morality, of the Abrahamic faith tradition, in the school context. It is here that the same-sex marriage movement as part of the ideology of hedonistic materialism moves to close this remaining source, which could contradict its own teaching of boundary-less sexuality. This is undertaken both in Government schools, in which legislation can much more easily intervene, as well as in private (largely faith-based) schools, with separate and overlapping strategies.

As noted, the Australian census indicates that about 70% of Australians express a religious affiliation. However, 65% of Australian school children attend Government Schools. Assuming (exaggeratedly) that all the children of religiously unaffiliated families (30%) attended Government Schools (and that birth-rates amongst religiously and non-religiously affiliated families were the same), there would still be more children from religiously identifying families than from religiously non-identifying families in Government schools. This is ostensibly particularly so in the case of ethnic minorities which arrive from strong religious backgrounds, but cannot afford to send their children to private schools.

Nowhere is it written in the legislation of the Australian States or concept underpinning Government schools, that they must *exclude* religion from their purview, and disallow the teaching of religion, whether as part of general curriculum or for those who want a religious education. Their task is to provide a *free* education for all children, who require it. To claim that no teaching of religion should be permitted in Government schools is an aggressive secularism which has no place in our culture, and is contrary to both the Victorian Charter of Rights and Responsibilities and section 116 of the Federal Constitution, which guarantee religious freedom.

Moreover, the National Curriculum Review Report (2014) specified as one of its recommendations that:

> ACARA *[Australian Curriculum, Assessment and Reporting Authority]* revise the Australian Curriculum to place more emphasis on morals, values and spirituality as outlined in the Melbourne Declaration, and to better recognise the contribution of Western civilisation, our Judeo-Christian heritage...

Notwithstanding this, the Government of Victoria after its election in 2014, excluded the program of Special Religious Instruction from school hours. Under this program different religious instruction bodies, Jewish, Christian, Muslim and other, had been given a school period lesson a week to teach students on a voluntary attendance basis. This program was driven out of school hours in Victorian Government schools from the beginning of the 2016 school year after the successfully lobbying of the Government by a secular-humanist organization, well in tune with the materialist-hedonistic ideology, called "Fairness in Religions in Schools" (FIRIS). FIRIS celebrated the Government decision as the "prize" for which it had been working.

The way in which the movement of hedonistic materialism proposes to deal with the private, faith-based schools is, in the present Victorian Government's agenda, to remove their exemptions under the "Equal Opportunity Act". The present legislation, which prohibits employers from discriminating against potential employees on grounds of gender or sexual orientation, contains exemptions. One of these exemptions is religious schools. This means that a religious school can presently decline to employ a teacher leading an openly homosexual lifestyle, as this is contrary to the values which it wants to model to its school community. Specifically, the Government's proposed change to this legislation will place the onus on a religious school to prove why the sexual lifestyle of a teacher is requisite for his or her role in the school. They are presumably willing to accept that the Scripture teacher must exemplify the morality which the school's religion prescribes, but a religious school will have to convince a secular tribunal why it makes any difference what the openly displayed sexual lifestyle of a mathematics teacher or school bursar makes to their functions. This secularist approach does not understand that a religious school environment teaches not only by word but also by example. In the American State of Massachusetts, where same-sex marriage has been legalized, a court recently compelled a Catholic school to hire a married homosexual as a cook in contradiction to the school's values and ethos. In the United Kingdom, under the regime of homosexual marriage, matters have gone further. Religious schools have been ordered to teach "sexual diversity" to their students on pain of closure.

There is a further measure, in the program of the Victorian Government, which effectively weakens the input of religion and its ethics from all schools, both Government and private, faith-based schools. This is the introduction of a new subject which will form a compulsory strand throughout schooling from the Foundation year to year ten. This is outlined in a document entitled "Learning about world views and religions". It proposes to teach children the basic premises of the distinct world religions Buddhism, Christianity, Hinduism, Islam, Judaism and secular humanism and rationalism. Significantly, instead of personal religion being taught by the believing teacher for the believing student, this is a relativizing comparative study. It is not taught from the standpoint of personal conviction but through a secular lens which evaluates different religions and secular humanism on the one plane. It is not religion which wells up out of personal belief and is made articulate through study. Rather it is a secular subject, taught from the outside looking in. The animus behind this subject is to teach "tolerance" and "respect". That sounds fine, but in fact it makes religion the problem, which a relativising study will neutralize, rather than the solution. Like other secular offerings on religion, it is not subject which is intended to nourish or strengthen personal spiritual identity. One does not approach the study of any one of religions offered in a smorgasbord (with secular humanism) as the teaching of *my* G-d, but rather as a kind of comparative ethnography.

Those who were comforted by the idea that this "General Religious Education" would replace "Special Religious Education (or Instruction)" are likely to be disappointed. The latter takes root in the soul, the former is just another academic subject. It does not make up the removal of Special Religious Instruction; rather it compounds the loss. The victory goes to the sixth world "religion" listed in the study program: secular humanism, in today's form, another species of hedonistic materialism. The G-d, Who prescribed traditional marriage, is to be put out of school, along with the soul of the child, which mirrors the moral compass of the banished G-d. They will return amongst much happiness for *all* humanity.

Further Reading

On the standpoint of universal ethics with regard to homosexuality

Rabbi M. M. Schneerson, 'Rights or Ills?', accessible at www.sie.org

S. D. Cowen, *The Theory and Practice of Universal Ethics – the Noahide Laws*, N.Y: Institute for Judaism and Civilization, 2014

On the psychological model of the human being

Viktor E. Frankl, *The Rediscovery of the Human – Basic Early Texts of Viktor E. Frankl*, 2nd Ed'n, translated by S. D. Cowen and Liesl Kosma, Melbourne: Institute for Judaism and Civilization, 2014. In this collection, see particularly the essay, "Ten theses concerning a 'person'"

On physiological and psychological dimensions of homosexuality

K.J. Zucker and S.J. Bradley, *Gender Identity Disorder and Psychosexual Problems in Children and Adolescents*, NY: Guilford Press, 1995

On the significance of the relationship of donor gametes to personal identity

Alana S. Newman, *The Anonymous Us Project: A Story-Collective on 3rd Party Reproduction*, NY: Broadway Publications, 2013

On the critique of mainstream psychology's doctrinal positions on homosexuality

Robert Spitzer, "Can Some Gay Men and Lesbians Change Their Sexual Orientation? 200 Participants Reporting a Change from Homosexual to Heterosexual Orientation", *Archives of Sexual Behavior*, Vol. 32, No. 5, October 2003, pp. 403-417

Stanton L. Jones and Mark A. Yarhouse, "A longitudinal Study of Attempted Religiously-Mediated Sexual Orientation Change", *Journal of Sex and Marital Therapy*, 37:404-427 (2011)

Stanton L. Jones and Mark A. Yarhouse, "Honest sex science", *First Things* (October, 2012)

On the practice of reparative therapy

Arthur Goldberg, *Light in the Closet*, Beverly Hills: Red Heifer Press, 2008

On the impact of new "sex education" on children (in areas other than homosexuality)

Miriam Grossman, *You're Teaching My Child What?*, Washington DC: Regnery Publishing Inc., 2009

www.ingramcontent.com/pod-product-compliance
Ingram Content Group UK Ltd.
Pitfield, Milton Keynes, MK11 3LW, UK
UKHW041414180426
11947UKWH00007B/129